A Shield against the Bomb

Ballistic Missile Defence in a Nuclear Environment

A Shield against the Bomb

Ballistic Missile Defence in a Nuclear Environment

A. Vinod Kumar

Vij Books India Pvt Ltd
New Delhi (India)

Published by

Vij Books India Pvt Ltd
(Publishers, Distributors & Importers)
2/19, Ansari Road
Delhi – 110 002
Phones: 91-11-43596460, 91-11-47340674
e-mail: vijbooks@rediffmail.com
web : www.vijbooks.com

CONTENTS

Preface   vii

Chapter - I   The Context   1

Chapter - II   The Evolution and Future of Strategic
                 Interception Technologies   13

Chapter III   Missile Defence and Nuclear Deterrence 38

Chapter IV   Offence-Defence Balance
                 and Missile Defence   55

Chapter - V   Missile Defence in the Southern
                 Asian Theatre   69

Chapter - VI   Conclusion   118

Index   123

PREFACE

It should not sound melodramatic when I say that I grew up watching sounding rockets.

The reference is not to the Diwali rockets unique to Indians, but of the *Nike-Apache* sounding rockets that used to be launched every Thursday from the launch pad of the Thumba Equatorial Rocket Launching Station (TERLS), a premier institution under the Indian Space Research Organisation (ISRO), located in Thiruvananthapuram at the southern tip of India. I was brought up in this campus (which was also the cradle of India's space programme), thanks to my father's employment at the Vikram Sarabhai Space Centre (VSSC), of which TERLS is an integral part or vice versa. The benefit of passing my childhood in this sprawling and historic campus was the unique opportunity to witness, at close quarters (though too young then to realise its enormity and importance), the early years of the Indian space programme (which I had also captured in my dissertation for the diploma programme in journalism at the Thiruvananthapuram Press Club), and also the honour of seeing in person some legendary figures like Dr V.R. Gowarikar, Dr U.R. Rao, Dr Brahm Prakash, Dr A.P.J. Abdul Kalam and Dr S.C. Gupta, to name a few, many of whom adorned senior positions in VSSC and ISRO, and resided among us in our community.

Being a part of the VSSC community had given my generation the privilege of experiencing the emotions and passions that were associated with the landmark ventures in those blossoming years of the Indian space programme, be it the enormous Satellite Launch Vehicle (SLV) projects ranging from SLV-3, (Augmented) ASLV, (Polar) PSLV to (Geo-synchronous) GSLV, or the sterling satellite family comprising of Indian Remote Sensing (IRS) satellites and the Indian National Satellite System (INSAT) series. We lived this phenomenon through their images and omnipresence in our daily lives—as small replicas that doubled up as mementoes adorning our showcases, the recycled rocket cones that served as ubiquitous letter boxes, and the larger-size ones that stood tall as mighty silhouettes across the sprawling VSSC campus.

These were the memories that dotted my mind when Dr C. Raja Mohan, as the convenor of the Indian Pugwash Society in 2004, assigned me with the task of preparing a working paper on ballistic missile defences as part of a Department of Atomic Energy project. One of the first things he then asked me to do was to understand the technology (of missile interception) before researching and writing about missile defences and its strategic dimensions. Many analyses of that time were seen to be loosely using missile defence nomenclatures like national missile defence (NMD) and theatre missile defence (TMD) without clear distinctions made of the varied technological concepts. Dr Raja Mohan, hence, sent me to Commander P.K. Ghosh, then a Senior Fellow at the Centre for Strategic Studies and Simulation, United Services Institution (USI), who had by then done some pioneering work in the Indian strategic community on missile defence. The topic was then just about dawning on the international scene (or rather making a reappearance in the post-Cold War strategic milieu) thanks to the decision of the then US President, George W. Bush, to reinvigorate the US missile defence programme (which was pursued in a limited form by the Clinton Administration) and pursue a multi-layered architecture that could intercept incoming missiles at all stages of its flight–boost, mid-course and terminal.

The working paper, though completed, could never be published. However, I was able to continue the research on missile defences after joining IDSA in May 2006. It was in December 2006 that I presented my first research paper on India and missile defence at IDSA. A month before my paper, India's Defence Research and Development Organisation (DRDO) announced, for the first time, that it was pursuing a BMD programme and that an interceptor test will be done in the next few weeks. The timing was purely coincidental though it was some sort of destiny that my research quest on BMD at IDSA went parallel with the DRDO's development track on this technological front.

This paper was readied for publication with the title *A Phased Approach to India's Missile Defence Planning*. While all the three international referees who reviewed the article termed it as path-breaking and innovative, my Director General decided to seek an additional opinion by sending it to a highly-placed official at DRDO, who, in turn, opined against its publishing. The apparent reason was that I was sceptical of the DRDO's claims of successful interceptions and had suggested the possibility of foreign systems coming into the Indian missile defence planning at some point of time in order to provide a nation-wide coverage. In the coming years, DRDO undertook many developmental tests of two endo-atmospheric interceptors—Prithvi Air Defence (which was projected as an exo-atmospheric system) and Advanced Air Defence (AAD)—and went on to declare them as ready for deployment. Subsequently, the agency also began work on a longer-range exo-atmospheric interceptor. As things stand today, the Indian government is moving ahead with the plan to acquire the S-400 missile/air interceptor from Russia. Moreover, the US government has included India in its Strategic Trade Authorisation list that could pave the way for even American missile defence platforms making their way into the Indian inventory in the not so distant future, thus validating the prognosis in the above-mentioned article.

Though my work on missile defence has been going on for more than a decade, I should be up-front in describing this monograph as a collation of my interim research findings. This is largely because the technology continues to evolve in terms of its capability and objective (of fool-proof interception), and the strategic dimensions of introducing this capability in a military environment, or a nuclear theatre, continues to remain at a nascent stage. Despite the technology being at various stages of development and numerous instances of accurate tracking and interception (often in simulated or ideal conditions), no military leader in charge of an operational strategic interception system or a technology leader overseeing such development can affirm with authority that a fool-proof shield has been put in place. Similarly, the strategic dimensions, including the implications of the mass pursuit of strategic interception technologies by the nuclear-armed states, continue to remain fluid or in evolutionary stages. In other words, no nuclear-armed power can make a compelling judgement on whether their missile defence capability has given them the decisive edge to deter their potential rivals, nor can a state confronted with a BMD-armed rival be assured that the shift to defensive posture has mitigated the possibility of future aggression or offensive posturing. On the contrary, as this study seeks to show, the possession of a BMD capability in a nuclear theatre has only added to its net deterrence capability, which could be converted into offensive posturing, thereby menacing the other actor(s) in the equation.

Having followed the evolution of this technology for close to two decades, I feel sufficiently equipped to explain the level of technological development and its role in the strategic ordering of the post-Cold War world, in what could be described as the third incarnation of the technology. This short-form monograph, hence, is a narrative covering three themes: (a) an overview of BMD technology and where it stands today, (b) a preliminary examination of the impact of BMD on nuclear deterrence using the framework of offence-defence balance, and (c) providing a case study of Southern Asia where BMD will influence and shape the nuclear deterrence dynamics in two nuclear dyads. Though a concise volume, it attempts to endow a comprehensive reflection on these themes, and give the reader an understanding of the technology, its strategic dimensions and a case study for an empirical experience.

The chapter on the evolution of strategic interception technologies traces its genesis from the post-War times and paces through the development trajectories of three epochs: the race between the superpowers on anti-ballistic missile (ABM) systems witnessed through the 1950s up till the early 1970s; the return of strategic interception concepts, this time in futuristic terms, through the Strategic Defence Initiative (SDI), popularly known as Star Wars, and espousing a battleground in outer-space; and the third incarnation in the post-Cold War years through concepts like NMD, TMD and numerous interceptor platforms that were supposed to add up as components of multi-layer and nationwide defences. The chapter encapsulates this technological survey and provides a holistic understanding of missile defence technologies, their current operational narratives as well as the futuristic concepts of interception and tracking technologies that are presently in the design tables.

The case study on Southern Asia imparts a comprehensive exposition of the deterrence calculus of the three nuclear-armed states, namely China, India and Pakistan, in order to locate the dynamics associated with the introduction of missile defence systems in the region. Being the dominant nuclear-armed state in the region, the Chinese strategic modernisation, which has been ongoing for over two decades, has been a subject of intensive focus, especially by Western analysts, who have attempted to interpret Chinese documents and official records to decipher the intricacies and direction of the modernisation exercise. Alongside the advent of new and advanced strategic delivery systems, the recent debates on the perceptible diversions or impulses in the doctrines and postures as seen in documents like the White Papers have been assessed in this chapter. The Chinese case has also been peculiar for its protracted opposition to missile defences and eventually ending up developing interceptors for a multi-layered architecture, a deceptive policy approach it has consistently taken in many strategic segments including on space weaponisation.

The India-Pakistan nuclear dyad, on the other hand, has seen a dynamic evolution of deterrence structures since the overt nuclearisation in 1998. The subcontinent was viewed by the international community as a nuclear flashpoint with the two nuclear-armed states indulging in numerous face-offs that could have escalated into full-fledged military hostilities, and potentially leading towards nuclear conflict. The four major crises since the 1998 tests and a sustained low-intensity conflict had caused tremendous pressures on the doctrinal and force structures in the dyad, and had driven the formulation of newer postural initiatives like India's Cold Start, as also revisions like the second-strike posturing by Pakistan after years of projecting first-strike intentions and ambiguous nuclear use thresholds. The introduction of tactical nuclear delivery systems and ballistic missile defence capability in this matrix is increasingly influencing the deterrence equations with the possibility of denial deterrence supplanting the existing calculus of retaliatory deterrence that has for long been shaped by offensive strategic forces. Around the time I was finishing the first draft of my monograph in early 2015, Lt. Gen. (retd) Khalid Kidwai, the former and long-time head of Pakistan's Strategic Plans Division (SPD), the custodian of its nuclear forces, had addressed the Carnegie Nuclear Policy Conference in March 2015 and validated the shift in the Pakistani strategy by using its tactical nuclear delivery and second strike forces as lynchpin of its denial deterrence posturing to match Indian's own pursuit of denial deterrence through its missile defence capability. I have captured these shifts in the chapter covering the Southern Asian case study.

The highlight of the monograph, however, is the sections that cover the strategic dimensions of missile defence, namely its implications for nuclear deterrence, the effects on the net offensive capability of the possessing state, its ability to provide a defensive edge to the possessor and the consequences thereof, among others. The USP of the two chapters covering this section is the usage of the offence-defence balance framework to explain these strategic dimensions. Offence-Defence theory propounds that when the offence has dominance in inter-state relations, it could lead to competition and war and when the balance favours defence, countries will be prompted to seek cooperation and peace. Though I did not attempt a discursive exploration of offence-defence theory in this study, I used its explanatory variable of offence-defence balance to determine the role and space that missile defence systems could occupy in a nuclear theatre. As the arguments in Chapter IV shows, the actual impact of missile defences could depend on how the possessing state projects this capability, especially in conjunction with its offensive forces or with a defensive intent, and how the rival state perceives this possession as either a stabilising act or a menacing one.

I first presented a paper on offence-defence balance and missile defence at IDSA in 2012, which was probably the first such paper then on the BMD-deterrence correlation using the offence-defence balance framework. I did not immediately proceed towards a publishing option as I felt the inferences made in these chapters form only a preliminary assessment of this correlation, and by using this particular framework. Further, I found it difficult to run the draft through the peer community in order to gain dialectical inputs to strengthen the paper further. The Delhi strategic community has a customary aversion towards such conceptual inquests. Neither could I access any opportunities to gauge insights on the paper from a constructive scholarly audience in the western world where such conceptual studies have greater traction. I hence use this monograph as a means to reach out to this international segment with the hope of gaining responses that will enable me to strengthen this quest and also to begin the next phase of this study. In the coming months, I will be exploring the means of using offence-defence theory to explain the BMD-deterrence correlation, especially by placing it as the 'technology' variable which has been extensively assessed in the offence-defence discourses.

****

This monograph is largely of 2015 vintage though many aspects of current technological developments and events pertaining to Southern Asia has been updated and explained sufficiently in the related chapters. Yet, there are four significant developments that have occurred when I was at advanced stages of revising the manuscript and could not be included in the relevant sections, mainly because these developments were still at their nascent stages and had potential to evolve further. The four issues are: (a) Russian President Vladimir Putin's unveiling of a series of new generation weapon systems claiming to have capabilities of global reach, the ability to negate BMD systems and the firepower to trigger a nuclear catastrophe; (b) India's decision to buy the Russian S-400 system amid concerns on whether the US will waive this purchase from its Russia-specific sanctions, while also adding India in the Strategic Trade Authorisation list; (c) Trump's (blurred) vision for the US BMD programme and its implications for the nuclear order; and (d) the Indian nuclear triad being declared as operational.

Putin's own Star Wars: Addressing the Russian Federal Assembly in March 2018, President Putin unveiled a series of new generation strategic weapons, which he claimed is 'invincible' and, more importantly, could overwhelm US missile defences. The speech echoed how the Russians view the American BMD edifice as completely devaluing their nuclear potential and undermining deterrence. Putin showcased the development of four systems: the *Sarmat* inter-continental missile to replace the Soviet-era *Voevoda* system; a manoeuvrable hypersonic glide vehicle with an unpredictable flight trajectory; a new sea-based unmanned submersible (termed as *Status-6* in some reports) that can move at great depths inter-continentally; and a nuclear-powered cruise missile that will be a low-flying stealth missile carrying a nuclear warhead. Each system, Putin insisted, had advanced attributes that were designed to negate the American missile interception systems.

Sample this: The *Sarmat* weighing over 200 tonnes will have a short-boost phase which, Putin claims, makes it difficult to be intercepted, and will be equipped with a broad range of nuclear warheads, including the hypersonic vehicle. The latter system, which Putin referred as *Kinzhal*, will be a nuclear-powered, high-speed platform that will fly at a speed 10 times faster than sound and will have the twin advantages of non-ballistic trajectories and high manoeuvrability that not just makes it overcome all defensive systems, but also could endow it with practically no range restrictions. The *Status-6* is touted as an "entirely new sea-based means to deliver a nuclear weapon," which, as Putin proclaimed in his video demonstrations, will be highly manoeuvrable and that "simply nothing in the world will be capable of withstanding them." Putin declared that an innovative nuclear power unit for this unmanned underwater vehicle had completed a test cycle in 2017, which makes it a nuclear-powered and nuclear-armed sea-based system when deployed. The cruise missile system, which was described as a "low-flying stealth missile carrying a nuclear warhead," is also powered by a small-scale heavy-duty nuclear energy unit that will ensure unlimited range, unpredictable trajectory and ability to bypass inceptors. Putin claimed this cruiser as capable of defeating any missile defence system with its supersonic speeds of Mach-20 and inter-continental range, thus creating a new generation of nuclear-armed cruise missiles.

By projecting the new systems as a pivot against the US missile defence architecture, Putin signalled the major recalibration of Russia's strategic posturing backed by a formidable upgrade of its nuclear arsenal. More importantly, the advent of a new generation of nuclear-powered and nuclear-armed weapon systems covering various classes of weaponry, and when deployed *en masse*, having the potential to ignite an arms race that may replicate or rival the earlier versions of great power competition. By citing the US BMD as a rationale for developing these systems, Putin essentially justified the long-standing Russian argument about US missile defences being de-stabilising and disturbing age-old deterrence equations based on mutual assured destruction (MAD). Yet, Russia's attempt to counter-balance through its own advanced interceptor systems (and proclaiming their global reach) complicates this calculus further, and in turn, opens space for global deterrence realignments (as described in Chapter IV). This display of advanced weaponry is a certain game-changer, though its actual contours may take further time to unravel and decisively impact global nuclear dynamics.

The Indian quest no longer indigenous: Since 2015, there have been reports of India seeking the S-400 systems from Russia. In recent months, India and Russia have moved towards finalising the purchase of 5 S-400 *Trimuf* systems, which, media reports suggest, will be a deal worth $ 5 billion. An untimely impediment to the fructification of this deal came in the form of the Countering America's Adversaries Through Sanctions Act (CAATSA) – a US Congress legislation that intends to sanction strategic and financial sectors in Russia, Iran and North Korea. The legislation empowers the US President to sanction the notified 39 Russian companies including key defence sector companies, which could also make third parties liable to sanctions if doing business with these entities. That the Almaz-Antey Corporation, the manufacturers of the S-400 system, also figures in this list made an Indian purchase vulnerable to US sanctions. With India reportedly conveying to the US that it will go ahead with the purchase, the matter had for many months bogged down governmental negotiations between the two to the extent that a scheduled 2+2 dialogue between their defence and foreign ministries in mid-2018 was postponed. Following pressure from the Trump administration, the Conference Committee of the US House of Representatives and Senate, in its final version of the National Defence Authorisation Act (NDAA) 2019, had recommended exempting India, Indonesia and Vietnam – key strategic partners in the Indo-Pacific – from Section 231 of CAATSA through an amendment. Accordingly, these countries could be allowed to buy Russian defence equipment without attracting sanctions, provided the US President certify that they have significantly reduced dependence on Russia and increased cooperation with the US. While such an exemption essentially paves the way for the S-400 deal to go through, there is still confusion on whether the Trump Administration has approved this exemption or is yet to take a final call.

However, the more significant, or rather intriguing, aspect is the Indian decision to buy the S-400 system. Since the time the DRDO publicized in 2006 its ongoing programme to develop missile defence systems for point and area defence and a potential nation-wide architecture, it had vociferously rejected any suggestions on the need for any foreign element in its indigenous programme, either as imported systems or technology development partnerships with other nations. But for notable exceptions like the Israeli *Greenpine* radar being used as primary tracking and guidance system for the two interceptors, the DRDO was largely averse to any external imprint in its plans. To that end, the agency was known to have discouraged the government from pursuing inter-governmental partnerships with the US despite missile defence being listed among the four core areas identified for strategic cooperation in the Next Steps in Strategic Partnership of September 2004.

On the other hand, it was evident that the political leadership has not been enthusiastic about the DRDO's claims of the two indigenously-developed systems being ready for deployment in the national capital and other strategic installations. Amid speculation that DRDO could have exaggerated the success of its developmental tests, the agency's efforts to make greater strides in the long-range interceptor programme was hindered when a test launch of the PDV in early 2014 failed to intercept the target. Since then, the agency has been keeping a low-profile about the development progress of the PDV and related programmes or about the deployment schedules for the PAD and AAD. The decision to buy the S-400 has to be viewed in this context, especially to understand the actual purpose of this acquisition, which, as of now, remains ambiguous. The S-400 is known for its twin capabilities in both air defence and missile defence roles and capable against faster missiles than what the PAD or AAD could do, though the interception range of *Trimuf* (30 km altitude and 400 km coverage) makes it only a super-efficient endo-atmospheric system, a goal tagged for the PAD system as well.

Does this imply the political leadership's lack of confidence in the operational scope/capabilities of the PAD and prefers a more efficient and proven system for its point and area defence applications? Or should this deal be seen as a political move of rapprochement with the Russians through the limited acquisition of a high-end system that could sharpen the defensive architecture? Will this, in some ways, imply that the government may not prefer a longer-range interceptor to deal with Chinese offensive forces and instead seek a riposte through a system that the Chinese are also in possession? These questions may continue to shroud the mystery as the Indian government hesitate to articulate its missile defence strategy or its role and space in the strategic deterrence mission. However, the interesting twist in this tale is the US decision, in the midst of the CAATSA debate, to include India in its Strategic Trade Authorisation list, usually reserved for allies. This measure, undoubtedly, is a signal from Washington that it could be open to transfer frontline BMD platforms including THAAD or Aegis to India in the coming future if India seeks cooperation in this realm. Besides the fact that this will mark a substantial shift in the US policy (of denying frontline BMD systems like Arrow to India in the past), the indications of a change in approach came during the S-400 imbroglio when various media reports suggested the possibility of US offering THAAD in order to wean India from the S-400 deal. Chapter V of this study also touches upon these eventualities as a natural progression in the Indian BMD programme.

Trump's BMD plan still in slow motion: Some experts who reviewed the recent version of my draft suggested that I have missed out on Trump's BMD policy. I had certainly attempted to understand the Trump administration's policy and approach towards missile defence, but could not find any significant impetus in the US BMD policy beyond what was expected from a Republican president. After what was seen as a 'stop-gap' allocation of $ 4 billion for 2017 and $ 8 billion for 2018, Trump made an initial budgetary request of $ 9.9 billion in funding for the Missile Defence Agency in 2019, which was subsequently raised to $ 11.5 billion. While many observers saw this as a decent hike in MDA funding, there is no clarity yet on Trump vision on this front. At the core of this gap is the prolonged delay in bringing out the Ballistic Missile Defence Review (BMDR), which was supposed to articulate how the MDA will fulfil the role and space envisaged for missile defences in the US National Security Strategy as well as in the nuclear mission as espoused in the Nuclear Posture Review (NPR). The NPR, for example, states that "the goal of limiting damage if deterrence fails in a regional contingency calls for robust adaptive planning to defeat and defend against attacks, including missile defence and capabilities to locate, track, and target mobile systems of regional adversaries."

The NDAA, for its part, promises greater investments in missile defence capabilities along with the development of a future architecture that will integrate BMD sensors with modernised SBIRS (space-based) satellites. In fact, a highlight of the enhanced allocation in the 2019 NDAA is the emphasis on boost-phase interception along with the call for space-based platforms, hyper-velocity missiles, directed energy systems and also cruise missile defences. This also gives us the reason to eagerly anticipate the BMDR, which might announce a new boost-phase intercept system to compensate for a critical gap in the multi-layered architecture after the winding up of Airborne Laser (ABL) by the Obama Administration. Based on the 2019 budgetary request, there are reports that the Trump administration might instruct the MDA to revive the space-based intercept platforms, which were the foremost elements in the Strategic Defence Initiative (SDI) of the 1980s. Though no one expects a substantial shift towards space-based interception capabilities, the Trump administration is likely to give a fillip to the directed energy programmes that could give a fresh life to many ongoing laser-based ventures which could supplant the primacy of kinetic energy platforms. This will mean greater funding for the laser-mounted projects pursued by the three services, many of which are described in Chapter II. Further, the advent of cruise-missile defence and hypersonic systems has the potential to accelerate the pace of US BMD programme towards a new technological generation.

India's progress towards a nuclear triad: The draft nuclear doctrine that was publicised by India's National Security Advisory Board (NSAB) in July-August 1999 had submitted that India's nuclear forces will be based on a "triad of aircraft, mobile land-based missiles and sea-based assets," with the objective of "establishing an effective, enduring, diverse, flexible and responsive force" in accordance with the concept of credible minimum deterrence. The draft also stated that "survivability of the forces will be enhanced by a combination of multiple redundant systems, mobility, dispersion and deception." A Cabinet Committee on Security (CCS) meeting of January 2003 reviewed the 'operationalisation' of the doctrine (draft) which implied that the pursuit of the triad has already been initiated. Since then, the primary pursuit of India's strategic programme, running through two decades, has been to establish the fundamental elements of the triad, spread across the three services. While the presence of Sukhoi-MKI and Mirage-2000 aircraft had ensured that the aircraft platforms were in place from the outset, the last decade was witness to many of the land-based missile systems—of the *Prithvi* and *Agni* family—maturing from developmental phases to operational deployment. From the tactical platforms initially conceived as part of the Integrated Guided Missile Development Programme (IGMDP) of the 1980s, the post-1998 evolution of the missile platforms, especially the *Agni* series, was their metamorphoses into core components of the strategic programme. The missile with the longest range among them, *Agni-V* (5000 km), after its first successful launch in 2012 had elevated India's nuclear deterrent from a status of existential deterrence to retaliatory deterrence. In fact, most of the *Agni* missiles have in the last few years gone through operational testing by the Strategic Forces Command, the custodian of India's nuclear forces.

Unlike the progress attained in the land and air assets of the triad, the naval leg proved a major technological challenge owing to the indigenous effort to construct a nuclear-powered and nuclear-armed submarine. What started as the Advanced Technology Vessel (ATV) in 1998 took close to two decades of developmental struggles for the INS *Arihant* to be eventually commissioned in 2016. On 5th November 2018, Prime Minister Narendra Modi declared the Indian nuclear triad as operational after the INS *Arihant* returned to base following the completion of the first deterrence patrol in the high seas, armed with the *Sagarika* K-15 nuclear-tipped ballistic missiles. A statement from the Prime Minister's Office (PMO) said: "Prime Minister Narendra Modi received today the crew of ship submersible ballistic nuclear (SSBN) INS *Arihant*. The submarine recently returned from its first deterrence patrol, completing the establishment of the country's survivable nuclear triad." While *Arihant*'s patrol was the formalisation of the triad, the full-fledged existence of a 'survivable' triad could take some more years as the next class of nuclear submarines - INS *Arighat* (and the S3 and S4) - swiftly move towards deployment on both the seaboards. This process needs to be buttressed by a robust command-and-control system that also includes a reliable and fool-proof delegation mechanism to the submarine commanders who will man the survivable leg of India's second-strike (and even pre-emptive) nuclear forces.

****

I have already described the thematic foundations of this short-form monograph and its essential character as a collation of my decade-long research on missile defence technology and its strategic dimensions. It also encapsulates my interim research findings on the missile defence-deterrence correlation. Based on this thematic variety, I have attempted to offer a concise, and yet elaborate, narrative on where missile defences stand today through their technological and strategic evolution. I will not claim this work as a coherent piece of literature on a specific structural construct of missile defence, but instead would like to propose it as a comprehensive text that will provide a cross-section of readers - including academics, policymakers and students of strategic studies - with a broad understanding on the technological concepts and strategic manifestations of missile defence. The inputs and responses I gain from readers will greatly help me in proceeding towards the next phase of this study, which will include greater theoretical interrogations and exploring newer dimensions like the impact of proliferation of missile defence on great power competition, the scope for cooperation and arms control (like the ABM treaty) and also how the advent of new generation technologies, especially in the realm of space-based platforms, may alter the character and strategic dimensions of missile defence globally.

I take this opportunity to thank Brig. Pradip Vij of Vij Publishers for showing interest in this short-form monograph and for swiftly working out a publishing plan. I am grateful to my senior at IDSA, Group Captain (Dr) Ajey Lele for being an inspiring figure in my research endeavours at the Institute. My gratitude is also due to Major General Alok Deb, the Deputy Director General at IDSA, and Prof. Shantanu Chakravarthi, Convenor of Institute for Foreign Policy Studies (IFPS), Kolkata (where I am a visiting faculty), for being beacons of support during the crucial phase of this manuscript preparation. This research endeavour would have been incomplete without the blessings of Dr C. Raja Mohan and Cmdr. P.K. Ghosh. Shanmughasundaram Sasikumar's dialectical interventions have been substantial in enriching the conceptual quests that I pursued for this study. Mukesh Jha of the IDSA library has been my dependable resource man when it came to accessing reference material and academic literature that has helped me throughout in this work. My family, both immediate and extended, and closest friends have continued to remain as my primary pillar of support through all productive and challenging phases in my research expeditions. My gratitude to all of them!

A. Vinod Kumar
vinujnu@gmail.com

Stop press: The Trump Administration unveiled its Ballistic Missile Defence Review on 17 January 2019.

Chapter - I

The Context

The [objective of] the Strategic Defence Initiative is to reduce the military effectiveness of nuclear weapons so dramatically that they become unreliable for modern warfare.

—George Keyworth,
US President's Science Advisor, 1983[1]

Two fundamental aspects come to mind when we talk about Ballistic Missile Defence (BMD), or its other incarnations variously known as Anti-Ballistic Missile (ABM) system or Anti-Nuclear Strategic Defence. The first is how major technological advancements in the military domain have been retorted to or riposted by counter-technological breakthroughs. History has often shown that a military technological invention can be challenged by a countervailing technology that can, if not mitigate its capability, provide for an alternative or response to diminish or neutralize the potency of the preceding technology. Only a handful of military inventions, like nuclear weapons, have escaped this trend. The case of ballistic missiles is no different. Right from the days of the German V-2 rockets, major military industrial powers have explored defences against rocketry and air-breathing platforms. Though air defence systems seemed an interim answer to ballistic threats, there was always an imperative of constructing a "shield against this sword" even if it implied a metaphorical scenario of "hitting a bullet with a bullet." A

---

1 George Keyworth, "Strategic Defence: A Catalyst for Arms Reduction," Remarks to the Third Annual Seminar of the Centre for Law and Nuclear Security, 23 June 1983, Charlottesville: University of Virginia.

challenging technological endeavour that it is, the evolution of interception technologies has been a laborious grind ever since the initial efforts began in the 1940s. However, the pursuit of defensive platforms for strategic interception came with the inherent potential to complicate the then evolving equations of nuclear deterrence which were driven by the technological primacy of offensive forces.

As the Cold War began consolidating in the 1950s, the superpowers were competing not just on offensive forces and strategic delivery platforms, but also on active defences with the objective of neutralizing the offensive forces of the rival or rendering it as ineffective as possible. The intensity of the competition and the desperation to gain an edge over the other was amplified by the Sputnik launch by the Soviet Union and the resultant "missile gap" perceived by the Americans. Both sides managed to develop and deploy various ABM platforms, even with nuclear-tipped interceptors. However, they soon realised the erosive effect these could have on the existing nuclear deterrence equation, based on the concept of mutual assured destruction (MAD). But more significant was the fact that the technology, in its initial evolution, was hardly considered fool-proof, especially against a massive nuclear attack, which the superpowers were then considered as probable, judging by the animosity that was enveloping in the Cold War frontlines.

The Anti-Ballistic Missile Treaty of 1972, negotiated as part of the Strategic Arms Limitation Talks (SALT-I), was a landmark instrument intended to provide a stabilizing effect and curtail at least one part of the strategic competition (on defensive platforms). However, the subsequent initiation of the Strategic Defence Initiative (SDI) in 1983, though seeming to echo at a superficial level what US President Ronald Reagan espoused— to make nuclear weapons obsolete—but in actual tenor and content depicted the American desperation to attain a decisive technological breakthrough in developing land- and space-based interceptors that could kill Soviet missiles in flight or in outer-space. While the SDI plan could not gain much traction beyond the initial conceptualisation and political proclamations, a host of baseline technologies conceived by the initiative were subsequently revived, and formed the formidable part of the US National Missile Defence (NMD) project of the 1990s, with some of them moving into advanced development and deployment in the subsequent, or contemporary, American multi-layer missile defence programme.

Notwithstanding the fact that the quest for an ultimate and fool-proof defensive system remains elusive, most of the advanced nuclear-armed nations are active in this pursuit—most prominently Russia, China, India, and Israel—all in different strategic settings, but with the common goal of raising the shield against nuclear weapons. Most of these baseline technologies and advanced platforms intend to create an array of interception, tracking, and surveillance applications on the ground, naval, and airborne platforms, with the space frontier, extensively being explored for parking the tracking and surveillance machinery. Some have matured and progressed into deployment, though in limited numbers, while a host of others are at various stages of development. Most of these platforms are expected to pass through greater technological augmentation and performance upgrade of life-cycles in the coming years. In this sense, the next few decades might witness operational maturity of many systems as well as the birth of new interceptor-vehicle concepts. The character and objectives of newer technologies or augmentations during the coming decades will inevitably shape the larger strategic environment and, in particular, the further evolution of nuclear deterrence.

The second aspect is about a related consequence: that is, what missile defences could do to strategic deterrence. Or, in other words, what does the advent of missile defences imply for the nuclear revolution? Will it trigger a counter-nuclear revolution which could diminish the primacy of nuclear deterrence? Or, will it create a strategic balancing that could preserve the existing nuclear symbolism? The general expectation about missile defences is that they should be capable of providing a credible defence against an attack with conventional or nuclear-armed missiles. However, there are different approaches to this basic premise. One is of the arms control or stability paradigm – that missile defences should be a hedge against surprise attack, should counter offence superiority, restrict the arms race, and reduce the salience and potency of nuclear weapons. The other is the nuclear war-fighting paradigm, which espouses that missile defences should give a strategic edge to nuclear forces, protect second-strike assets against a pre-emptive attack, add to the net deterrence value of nuclear forces, and deter all forms of aggression—conventional and nuclear. In other words, the fundamental point of debate is whether missile defences could complement the nuclear revolution by enhancing the deterrence of nuclear forces, or whether it could make nuclear weapons obsolete by providing a formidable defence against their use.

This techno-strategic binary underlines the invariable paradoxes associated with the pursuit of missile defences, which stimulates not just enigma and self-doubt but also multiple approaches, amongst both the positivist proponents as well as the sceptics of this technology. On the one hand, there are positivists who look at missile defences as a means to protect against total annihilation, render nuclear weapons redundant, and lead to their gradual obsolescence, and eventually prevent war and destruction, the classic example being Ronald Reagan's approach propounded through the SDI. Reagan "strategic concept", according to Stephen Cimbala, conceived of a scenario when defences based on non-nuclear technology might eventually displace offensive nuclear weapons, as the superpowers would disarm down to zero and build non-nuclear defences.[2] With nothing much to accomplish, the remaining nuclear weapons would no longer present a threat to the defences or targets they were designed to protect, leading to "swords being sheathed and shields becoming triumphant." Then, there are the reformists who are optimistic about missile defences as a means to reframe the paradigm of retaliation and mutual destruction, by placing defences as the fulcrum of the deterrence optics. The other section represents more of negativism and self-doubt—whether the technology will be reliable, credible, and

---

2   Stephen J. Cimbala, *Clausewitz and Escalation: Classical Perspective on Nuclear Strategy*, New York: Frank Cass, 1991.

durable; whether the shield will triumph over the sword; whether a bullet can quite always hit another bullet with certainty; and whether reliability on defences could be a sustainable proposition on which huge stakes could be placed, especially if one invading rocket that passes through the defences could trigger a global catastrophe.

A prominent example of these paradoxes is the SDI—what it intended to achieve (rather, the divergent conceptions about its objectives) and what it ended up as. The SDI was supposedly driven by Ronald Reagan's "strategic concept", whose political principle was of "transcending nuclear deterrence" and "reducing the risk of nuclear war."[3] The SDI was also propounded as a moral obligation "to save lives and not to avenge them" by the creation of a world where nuclear weapons were supplanted by defences based on non-nuclear technology. Accordingly, they propounded the belief that the SDI would make nuclear weapons obsolete, eventually forcing nuclear powers to disarm down to zero, with non-nuclear defences becoming the core defensive posture. Yet, American strategic planners and their core adversaries saw the SDI as the "Star Wars" plan wherein the space frontier would be the battleground for American and Soviet troops to fight out the next phase of the Cold War. The "Star Wars" concept perpetuated popular fiction and imagination about space weapons, laser systems, and futuristic technologies alien to the generation of the 1980s. For the American military-scientific-industrial caucus, the SDI was about reviving what was hindered by the ABM Treaty of 1972—the search for superlative strategic interceptors that could provide comprehensive homeland defence to US territory and European allies from Soviet missiles. To the Soviets, the SDI was about a destructive arms race that could bleed them to economic collapse and political demise. While many of the baseline technologies that were conceived as part of the SDI have been revived in subsequent BMD programmes, the original idea of "making nuclear weapons obsolete" has remained a fallacy.

---

3   Text of President Reagan's SDI speech of 23 March 1983, available at: http://www.atomicarchive.com/Docs/Missile/Starwars.shtml, accessed September 2015.

At a more holistic level, one notices three key drivers that favour the development and deployment of missile defence: (a) the security imperative—where a domino effect is created when the acquisition of strategic defences by one nuclear-armed state causes a security dilemma and prompts its rival(s) to pursue the technology as a security requirement; (b) the technological imperative—where an offensive technology has to be riposted by a defensive one so as to ensure that offence forces do not permanently maintain superiority; (c) the strategic imperative—where the nuclear environment demands a counter-revolution that could provide for a technological means to counter a nuclear attack, and to provide defence against irrational and insatiable actor(s).

Missile defences, in fact, propel many structural questions regarding their impact on the nuclear revolution, especially their ability to influence or alter the primacy of nuclear weapons. Deterrence, according to Lawrence Freedman, "pervades the logic that an enemy will be dissuaded from using a particularly obnoxious weapon with a threat of reprisal in kind."[4] What could missile defences do to this notion? Can it transform this notion in any manner, especially when there is a defence against an obnoxious weapon, or when the ability for reprisal could be used for pre-emption? Can a nuclear attack be countered by defending against a first strike? Can an enemy be deterred by the perception that defences could negate its attack or that the nuclear-armed adversary could engage in massive retaliation if it could defend its second-strike assets with its missile defences, effectively or even modestly? Conversely, will a state holding missile defences be emboldened to attack a nuclear-armed rival with the belief that a retaliatory strike could be defended or countered? In other words, are missile defences expected to exert costs on an attacker or enhance incentives for the first strike? There are many such questions regarding the effects missile defence could have on the nuclear environment.

---

4 Lawrence Freedman, *The Evolution of Nuclear Strategy* (London: Macmillan, 1989).

Such questions have perturbed strategic planners and deterrence theorists since the advent of strategic defences in the 1950s and 1960s, and have remained as enduring conceptual complexities for nuclear strategy, thanks to the dynamic evolution of the technological trajectory—be it the early competition between the superpowers or the constraints imposed on strategic interception platforms by the ABM Treaty; the revival-of-sorts driven by the SDI; and the subsequent post-Cold War rebirth of BMD systems. In fact, four major epochs pertaining to nuclear politics in post-War history could be used as narratives on the complex inter-relationship between nuclear weapons, missile defence, and deterrence.

The first was the budding competition between the USA and the Soviet Union in the late 1950s and the 1960s to develop ABM systems as a means to intercept long-range strategic missiles of each other. This was a period when the Americans initially braced for a Soviet first-strike with the strategy of *massive retaliation*, and later, realizing an offensive parity and vulnerability with the Soviet forces, came around to a posture of *assured destruction*. With *mutual assured destruction* (MAD) bolstering deterrence in an equation of *mutual vulnerability,* the advent of ABM systems threatened to destabilize this arrangement. Hence, both countries agreed on the ABM Treaty which restricted the development of defences,[5] so as to maintain mutual vulnerability for credible deterrence. Nonetheless, the intense race for global dominance and the lack of trust convinced both nations on the need to ensure that the other does not exploit a mutual vulnerability in its favour.

Despite the restrictions imposed by the ABM Treaty, both countries sustained their efforts to develop defensive shields, best embodied by the SDI and similar endeavours on the Soviet side. While President Reagan sought to project the SDI as a progressive

---

5 Initially two ABM deployments, one for the capital and one at another site, were allowed to be within a radius of 150 km over designated areas where not more than 100 launchers and six radars were permissible. The 1974 protocol to the Treaty restricted ABMs to a single area. While the Soviets maintained *Galosh* outside Moscow, the USA deployed the *Safeguard* in Grand Forks, which it closed down in 1976.

venture that could eventually lead to a nuclear weapon free world, the Soviets saw in it a blatant challenge to the MAD equation and American efforts to plug vulnerability, which, it feared, could give Washington the wherewithal to veer towards pre-emptive options against Soviet offensive forces. Though the SDI went down with the Cold War, the American pursuit of interception technologies continued in the form of National Missile Defence (NMD), and, later, the Ballistic Missile Defence programme.[6]

The third instance was when President George W. Bush withdrew from the ABM Treaty and called for new concepts of deterrence that rely on both offensive and defensive forces, arguing that "deterrence can longer be based solely on the threat of nuclear retaliation."[7] Along with his national BMD deployment plan, President Bush announced a Ground-based Mid-Course Defence System (GMDS) in the Czech Republic and Poland to defend against missiles from "rogue states". However, such deployment in former Warsaw Pact states was seen as a direct negation of the Russian, and also the Chinese nuclear deterrent. Upon intense opposition, the Obama Administration revamped the plan to a mobile deployment—though that did not stop the Russians and Chinese from pursuing their own BMD systems along with modernising their offensive forces.

The fourth instance, a contemporary and post-Cold War scenario, is of a handful of nuclear weapon states—mainly the US, Russia, China, India and Israel—that are in possession or actively pursuing strategic interception platforms, and seeking to alter the deterrence calculus with their nuclear adversaries or competitors

---

6 Before President Bill Clinton launched the NMD programme to develop multi-layer interception systems, President George H.W. Bush initiated a rudimentary version called the Global Protection against Limited Strikes (GPALS). In 2002, President George W. Bush sanctioned the BMD programme to develop interceptors for a layered architecture, with initial deployment by 2004.

7 Remarks at the National Defence University, Washington, 1 May 2001. Text of speech available at: http://www.fas.org/nuke/control/abmt/news/010501bush.html, accessed April 2012.

through the deployment of missile defence.[8] However, despite the varying levels of development and deployment progress, there is a uniform lack of clarity among their doctrinal administrators on what role missile defence systems may end up playing in their deterrence structures or on their potential implication for deterrence stability, especially how their adversaries will respond to these systems.

The common characteristic of these events is the indomitable unease of nuclear-armed states in keeping their vulnerabilities open and the enduring quest to plug them even while enhancing the potency of their nuclear deterrents as a strategic continuum. Missile defence has, invariably, emerged as the technological answer to this pursuit, but with the inherent potential of undermining existing deterrence equations. During the Cold War, ABM systems were perceived to be destabilizing the MAD equation by mitigating vulnerabilities in favour of the country possessing this capability and thus endowing it with the advantage to strike first and defend against retaliation. When both superpowers attained this capability, they recognized its detrimental impact on deterrence stability, and as a cause for a security dilemma. Concepts of assured destruction and massive retaliation continue to remain as key deterrent postures of nuclear powers, assuming mutual vulnerability as an established norm for nuclear stability—missile defence has emerged in this setting as a certain game-changer. Though the numerical increase of offensive forces was initially considered as a means to counter defences and sustain the efficacy of assured destruction, the increasing

---

8   As a nation with undeclared nuclear weapon capability and no nuclear-armed neighbours, Israel's defences are more of a theatre-level character, and may not immediately take a strategic dimension or impact nuclear deterrence in the region. Though some members of the North Atlantic Treaty Organisation (NATO) are in possession of systems capable of BMD applications, the European theatre is largely covered by the Medium Extended Air Defence System (MEADS) and the European Phased Adaptive Approach (EPAA), which entails the deployment of US sea-based and theatre defence systems. For an overview, see Randall M. Hendrickson, "European Phased Adaptive Approach (EPAA) Ballistic Missile Defence: A Technical Overview," May 3–4, 2012, at: http://photos.state.gov/libraries/russia/231771/PDFs/EPAA%20Technical%20Overview%20ENG.pdf, accessed April 2012.

effectiveness of missile defence platforms (rate of interceptions during development tests), howsoever questionable or doubted, have prompted other nuclear powers to contemplate a similar balancing. As we visualize a scenario where nuclear powers will retain their offensive forces as a primary deterrent while also pursuing missile defence coverage, the resultant impact could push the contours of deterrence to a conceptual and systemic transformation.

This being the general backdrop of the dialectics on missile defence, this monograph devotes its analysis to the transforming dimensions of this technology and the implications for deterrence when missile defence operates in a nuclear environment. Discerning the impact of missile defences on nuclear deterrence, though, remains an age-old puzzle. While one aspect of this relationship that needs to be investigated could be the implications of an asymmetric equation where only one actor advantageously possesses this technology, the other imperative is to ascertain whether missile defences could contribute to deterrence stability when major nuclear states gain some form of equity on this front. That, however, requires analysis of the deterrence implications created by missile defence when it adds to the net capability of strategic forces and, in the process, generates either comprehensive defence dominance or, possibly, an offence advantage. An environment of offence dominance, which prevails as a constant feature, always sustains the possibility of a recurring security dilemma for the adversary, prodding it to acquire similar or superior capability—one that can overwhelm its rival, thus consistently driving competition.

A suitable framework to approach these questions would be the offence-defence theory and its determinant, the offence-defence balance. The fundamental premise about offence-defence balance and the explanatory theory is that when an offence has dominance in inter-state relations, it could lead to competition and war; and when the balance favours defence, countries will be prompted to seek cooperation and peace. This paradigm has been used from the Clausewitzian times to explain the significance of both offence defence dominance scenarios in conventional warfare. In the nuclear age, theorists like Robert Jervis, Duncan Snidal, and Stephen Van Evera, among others, have expanded this premise into a theoretical framework to espouse the concepts of security dilemmas and strategic stability. Most of these conceptions, though, explore the consequences for warfare (relative costs and benefits of attacking and defending) when either offence or defence dominates with the generic argument that the superiority of offence could perpetuate war and destruction whereas the dominance of defence could lessen security dilemmas, reduce arms races, and enhance the security of states. Theorists like Jervis and Van Evera have also used technology as a variable to analyse offence-defence balance and implications for the security dilemma.

This study propounds the assumption that missile defence will be a suitable technological variable to explain the multiple dimensions of offence-defence balance in a nuclear environment. It undertakes a preliminary conceptual analysis of what a strategic environment dominated by defence could entail for nuclear deterrence: whether an asymmetric possession of missile defence could be menacing to the rival or compound its security dilemma; whether the possessor derives an offensive advantage to net deterrent capability and accrue incentives to strike first; whether it holds the benefits of defence superiority by denying the rival's capability to pre-empt or strike first and yet secure its retaliatory capabilities intact; and whether a potential parity of strategic interception capabilities will facilitate a more stable equation that could lead to nuclear weapons being made redundant or their primacy reduced, and as a consequence providing for deterrence stability and, probably, total elimination.

Aiding these analytical inquisitions are the following questions: Will missile defences favour a defensive balancing or will they enable (or complicate) deterrence by adding to a net offensive capability? How can an offence or defence balance be distinguished in a strategic environment influenced by missile defences? If BMD favours offence dominance for nations possessing it, is competition and arms race a natural military outcome? If so, can this competition be managed through a new stability equation as a political outcome? This volume uses Southern Asia as a case study to understand the evolving nature of missile defence in a nuclear environment. This region is chosen for the presence of the two nuclear dyads—China and India, and India and Pakistan – and for the fact that nuclear deterrence itself has not sufficiently consolidated in this region with missile defences adding to the incertitude and inchoate churning of strategic capabilities and interactions. Such a theatre promises to give greater insights on the implications for deterrence when BMD systems are introduced.

This study propounds two key arguments: (a) missile defences are instruments of security maximization that could accentuate offence dominance by adding to the net offensive capability of strategic forces; (b) a (mutual) defensive deterrence arrangement can emerge between BMD-possessing nuclear weapon states as a means to deterrence stability and encouraging arms control. In order to understand the actual impact of missile defence, the study starts with a survey of the evolution of BMD technology and the trajectory of developmental progress which could throw light on the extent of capabilities and intentions.

CHAPTER - II

THE EVOLUTION AND FUTURE OF STRATEGIC INTERCEPTION TECHNOLOGIES

The initial forays in interception technology started with the German *Wasserfall* and followed by the Soviet's *Berkut* and American projects like *Wizard* and *Thumper* in the 1940s—all strategic air defence systems with minimal anti-ballistic missile capability. The actual work on the ABMs started with the US *Project Plato* and the Soviet's "A" in the early 1950s,[1] propelled by the nuclear competition between the superpowers and their quest to develop defences against the other's longer-range nuclear-tipped missiles. While the Americans launched their Nike-Zeus and later the Nike-X programmes in the 1950s and 60s,[2] the Soviets followed suit with the A-35 ABM,[3] deployed around Moscow with the thermonuclear-tipped

---

1 For an overview of the early ABM programmes, see "Missile Defence: The First Sixty Years", Missile Defence Agency Backgrounder, 15 August 2008, www.mda.mil/mdalink/pdf/first60.pdf, accessed April 2012.

2 Endo-atmospheric ABMs are shorter-ranged and intercept their targets within Earth's atmosphere (100 miles or Karman line). The disadvantages are its limited range, and limited decision and tracking time. Exo-atmospheric missiles are high-altitude ones with longer ranges, and undertake interception outside Earth's atmosphere. Besides more decision and tracking time, they defend larger areas, while the need for heavier systems would be a disadvantage.

3 A. Karpenko, "ABM and Space Defence," *Nevsky Bastion*, No. 4, 1999, at http://www.fas.org/spp/starwars/program/soviet/990600-bmd-rus.htm, accessed April 2012.

Galosh A-350 interceptor. Following the *Galosh's* deployment, the US developed the *Sentinel* system and later re-oriented it into the *Safeguard* system to be deployed by the late 1960s. As this race between the superpowers began to spiral along with the one on offensive forces, the realisation dawned on both sides that defensive platforms may directly impact the evolving deterrence equations that were centred on the offensive build-up. As a matter of fact, the rationale propounded for the ABM Treaty was that effective limits on anti-missile systems would be a "substantial factor in curbing the race in strategic offensive arms."[4] In fact, the coming into force of this treaty did not hinder both countries from continuing the development of ABM technologies, which remained an ongoing quest as the risk of keeping vulnerabilities open remained a strategic concern throughout.[5] Indeed, the American leap towards the SDI a decade after the ABM treaty seemed intrinsically influenced by an enduring security dilemma driven by the belief that the other side continues to gain a strategic edge in offensive forces along with maintaining the defensive shield, irrespective of varied assessments about its efficacy.[6]

---

4   See Arms Control Association, "The Anti-Ballistic Missile (ABM) Treaty at a Glance, August 2012, at: https://www.armscontrol.org/factsheets/abmtreaty, accessed September 2016.

5   Most American assessments during the period hinted at the Soviets gaining an advantage in strategic forces despite the latter's own apprehensions on the reliance on the existing ABM systems to counter a US strike. The Americans felt that the Soviets are enhancing their counter-force capabilities, improving the survivability of offensive forces and adding to passive defences. Thus, the US defence establishment assumed that Soviet nuclear forces were potent enough despite the limitations imposed by SALT-I and the ABM Treaty. See US Congress, Office of Technology Assessment, *Ballistic Missile Defense Technologies*, OTA-ISC-254,Washington DC: U.S. Government Printing Office, September 1985.

6   The factors attributed to this condition could be apprehensions caused by the Soviets upgrading of the *Galosh* system in 1978, and plans for an advancement by 1980s (ABM-135) which implied ongoing work on defensive shields. Adding to this could have been the Soviet decision to retain both ABM deployments even as the US withdrew the Safeguards system at the ICBM site.

SDI to NMD

The need to overcome the strategic stalemate created by the MAD equation was reflected in President Reagan's March 1983 speech in which he underlined the need to develop an advanced and futuristic ABM architecture that would make "nuclear weapons obsolete", and shift the nuclear balance in its favour. More importantly, the SDI heralded the development of a new generation of baseline ballistic missile defence (BMD) technologies and conceived new architectural models, many of them continuing to be pursued even today, and likely to reflect through the numerous kill medium and delivery platforms of many upcoming projects. The major emphasis of the SDI was on space-based interceptors (SBI) for which concepts like Smart Rocks (Garage satellites with multiple interceptors) and Brilliant Pebbles (constellation of smaller interceptor satellites) were envisioned. The SDI conceptualized a four-layered architecture called Strategic Defence System (SDS), consisting of ground-, sea-, space-based and airborne components,[7] delineating the interception stages of a missile—boost, post-boost, mid-course and terminal phases—which continue to be the fulcrum of contemporary BMD architectures.

Of all, the *Boost Phase* is considered to be the most ideal interception phase if technologies can rise up to the challenge of intercepting a missile at source—an effort yet to fructify in dependable or credible terms. Boost Phase Interception (BPI) happens in the first few minutes after launch when the missile would have a slowly changing altitude and large infrared signature while clearing Earth's gravity and would be easily trackable even as the midcourse decoys are prevented by destroying the missile early in its flight. The SDS planned a *Post-Boost Phase*, which in current parlance is the early-ascent stage: a phase where the warhead/re-entry vehicles (several in a MIRVed ICBMs) move independently outside the Earth's atmosphere, enabling the sensors to track their flame signatures and directly target before they are dispersed. The *Mid-Course,* considered the most gruelling engineering

---

7   For a detailed analysis of the SDS, see Sanford Lakoff, *Strategic Defence in the Nuclear Age* (Westport: Praeger Security International, 2008).

endeavour, is the phase where long-range missiles exit and travel the large distance outside Earth's atmosphere before re-entry and endows the largest "window" for interception (over 20 minutes for an ICBM) with the missile following a predictable trajectory. However, by this time, the re-entry vehicle will be independent and aided by decoys which make the tracking difficult. In the *Terminal Phase,* the warhead would re-enter the Earth's atmosphere and be in its final journey towards the intended target. Though the task of discriminating decoys from the warhead would be easier, interception is critical in this stage as a failed interception would mean the warhead fulfilling its intended task of destruction.

A series of systems were planned in the SDS phase, which included space-based sensors and interceptors, like the Space-Based Interceptor (SBI), the Exo-atmospheric Re-entry Vehicle Interceptor System (ERIS), and the High Endo-atmospheric Defence Interceptor (HEDI)—concepts that later metamorphosed into the Ground-Based Interceptor (GBI) and Theatre High Altitude Area Defence (THAAD), though the space-based interceptor still remains in the realm of creative imagination. As for kill-vehicles, the SDS attempted various mediums, including nuclear-tipped, kinetic, and directed energy (laser and particle beams) sources. Considering the collateral destruction potential of nuclear warheads, the SDI shifted focus to Kinetic Kill Vehicles (KKV) which destroys the warhead by velocity collision (hit-to-kill).

A significant part of KKV ventures was concentrated on two programmes—*Brilliant Pebbles* and *Smart Rocks,* intended to raise space-based platforms for a mid-course and boost-phase interception. While *Smart Rocks* aimed at deploying huge satellite garages to host a large number of KKVs, *Brilliant Pebbles* relied on "singlets" or small, self-contained kinetic interceptors orbiting the space in large numbers.[8] The shift to *Brilliant Pebbles* came

---

8   From an initial plan for a 4000-strong constellation, the *Brilliant Pebbles* was to have over a lakh Pebbles in outer space. See "Brilliant Pebbles" in www. missilethreat.com/missiledefencesystems/id.13/system_detail.asp, accessed October 2009; also see "Missile Defence, Space Relationship, and the Twenty First Century", *Independent Working Group Report, 2009 Report,* The Institute for Foreign Policy Analysis, Inc., at http://www.ifpa.org/pdf/

after a debate on the vulnerabilities associated with large satellite garages, which could be sitting ducks for Anti-Satellite (ASAT) weapons. Smaller and autonomous interceptors were seen as a better option in terms of asset safety and costs. It was also felt that *Brilliant Pebbles* can be used for mid-course interception if backed by a constellation of low-orbit satellites, christened the *Brilliant Eyes*. However, concerns over the violation of the ABM Treaty diminished threats from ICBMs with the end of Cold War, and President Bill Clinton's scepticism led to *Brilliant Pebbles* being wound up subsequently. Nonetheless, many of its space components were considered ideal for future architectures. On the other hand, a series of theatre defence projects were reoriented from SDI concepts, which included the THAAD, *Patriot* (Phased Array Tracking to Intercept of Target), and the *Arrow* system.

The Soviets, for their part, also tried to catch up with this tit-for-tat race. During the 1970s, Moscow pursued a new high-altitude ABM system, the A-135, which was equipped with nuclear-tipped interceptors, and went into deployment in 1989. The twist to this competition, however, was the technological strategy the Soviets adopted during the peak SDI years, by shifting focus to strategic air defence systems with innate ABM capability and inherently lower costs. In the years after the Cold War ended, Russia thrived on this niche to develop a new generation of advanced air defence systems which, they claimed, were on par with lower-end American theatre defence systems.

Though the relevance of SDI diminished with the collapse of Soviet Union, the technological quest in this domain was sustained by the US Global Protection against Limited Strikes (GPALS) programme, launched by President George Bush (Sr.) in 1991, with a focus on ground-based defences against limited missile threats and accidental launches in what could be termed as a de-escalation period.[9] The first-ever wartime missile defence

IWG2009.pdf, accessed September 2016.

9   US Congress, House of Representatives, 102nd Congress, 1ˢᵗ Session, *Missile Defence Act of 1991*, Part C of National Defence Authorization Act for Fiscal Years 1992 and 1993: Conference Report to Accompany H.R. 2100, Report 102–311.

operation occurred during this period when US *Patriots* attempted to intercept Iraqi *Scuds* in the first Gulf War. That only 9 percent of those interceptions were successful hardly affected BMD missions and instead pushed the case for more effective ground-based defences against theatre-level threats. Though President Clinton initially retained the GPALS, he later sanctioned the development of a limited nationwide defence (NMD) project, consisting of ground-based interceptors, theatre defence projects like Patriot Advanced Capability (PAC-3) and THAAD, and the Airborne Laser (ABL), for a boost-phase interception.[10] His successor, George W. Bush, reinvigorated these projects and announced a robust BMD deployment plan by 2004. After withdrawing from the ABM Treaty, he re-designated the NMD programme as Ground-based Midcourse Defence System (GMDS), though this could not be declared operational till 2005 owing to consecutive test failures.[11] The year of revival proved to be 2006 when many programmes showed signs of optimistic progress, prompting President Bush to plan the first foreign deployment of GMDS in the Eastern European.

The US missile defence plans, however, hit new roadblocks with President Barack Obama who had, in his campaign days, declared his scepticism towards BMDs, and had promised to deploy only proven technologies while cancelling the money-guzzlers.[12] After an intense debate, Obama withdrew from the Eastern European BMD in September 2009 and, instead, backed a mobile deployment, termed as the European Phased Adaptive Approach (EPAA), consisting of the *Aegis* Standard Missile (SM) 3/6, THAAD and PAC-3. Avowed to the disarmament cause, Obama perceived BMDs to be destabilizing (unlike the earlier

---

10 James M. Lindsay and Michael E. O'Hanlon, *Defending America*, Washington DC: The Brookings Institution, 2001.

11 Bradley Graham, "U.S. Missile Defence Test Fails", *Washington Post*, 16 December 2004; "US Missile Defence Test Ends in Fiasco", *AFP*, Washington, 15 February 2005.

12 See Obama for America, "A 21st Century Military for America: Barack Obama on Defence Issues," www.barackobama.com/pdf/Defence_Fact_Sheet_FINAL.pdf, accessed March 2009.

Reagan line of thought), and expressed the desire to curb many technological endeavours that could trigger an arms race with other great powers like Russia and China. Nevertheless, the pursuit of baseline technologies flourished, driven by the fact that missile technologies entwined with weapons of mass destruction (WMD) continued to proliferate globally and remained the foremost threat.

Current Baseline Technological Scene

(a) US BMD pursuits:

The ongoing phase of BMD technology development in the US architecture is an assortment of baseline technologies pursued since the Clinton and George W. Bush years. While some projects got revamped and some terminated, the key ones are at advanced stages of maturity, both in terms of development and deployment, and holding the promise of interception capabilities for a layered defence. For the terminal or theatre defence phase, there are three notable systems—the PAC-3, *Arrow-2* and the THAAD—all of which have moved into deployment. An improvement of the *Patriot* air defence system, PAC-3 has a 15 km+ range at Mach-5 speed and is considered ideal for defence against slower, low-flying missiles.[13] By the early half of this decade, over 700+ PAC-3s have been deployed, with some in countries like Israel, Japan, and Turkey. The *Arrow-2*, a US-Israeli joint venture, has a higher altitude range (90 km) as the two-stage solid-fuel system could intercept at the upper segments of the Earth's atmosphere.[14] Its main attraction is the *Elta's Greenpine* fire control radar that can detect and track targets at a distance of over 500 km.

---

13 The PAC-3 is single-stage mobile system with a hit-to-kill capability and can carry 16 missiles at a time. For more on PAC-3, see "Lockheed Martin *Patriot* PAC-3," *Directory of U.S. Military Rockets and Missiles*, at www. designation-systems.net/dusrm/app4/pac-3.htm, accessed March 2013.

14 With a Mach-9 velocity, the *Arrow* 2 is a lethal endo-atmospheric ABM, which uses an initial burn for a vertical launch, a secondary burn to sustain its trajectory and destroys missiles through a blast fragmentation warhead. See www.israeli-weapons.com/weapons/missile_systems/surface_missiles/ Arrow/ Arrow.html, accessed March 2013.

While the PAC and *Arrow-2* operate as endo-atmospheric systems, the THAAD system with a 100 km+ range has extended theatre defence capability by intercepting missiles beyond the endo-atmospheric zone, or at the fringes of the Earth's atmosphere.[15] Deployment started in 2009 when the US Army incorporated six batteries with more than 100 interceptors into its ranks. Having gone through allied deployment in Turkey and the United Arab Emirates, THAAD is now in the news for its arrival in South Korea in May 2017 as the primary shield against short- and medium-range missile threats from North Korea. While emerging as the theatre defence mainstay for the US forces and its key allies, an Extended Range (ER) version is currently being developed to counter hypersonic missiles.[16] The MDA is now reportedly formulating a new, lower-tier architecture, with extended early-ascent or late-descent applications through a combination of Arrow-3, THAAD-ER, and Aegis Standard Missile-6, which are termed as "low-intensity, high-demand assets" that could offset the delay in achieving a credible mid-course interception capability.[17]

The flagship project of US BMD is the GMDS, which is being developed to protect against long-range missiles during the mid-course phase and is supposed to be the only partially operational system that could intercept ICBMs in outer-space. Its primary vehicle is the Ground-Based Interceptor (GBI),[18] which relies on a variety of satellites and radars (like Cobra Dane, X-band and AN/SPY-1) for launch warning, tracking, targeting and discrimination (of re-entry vehicle from decoys). Bogged by

---

15 The THAAD entered the manufacturing phase in 2000. A single-stage rocket with thrust vectoring to boost it beyond burn out, the THAAD system operates in conjunction with the X-Band radar. See www.defencelink.mi/specials/missiledefence/tmd-thaad.html, accessed March 2009.

16 Inside Missile Defence, Vol. 21 (9), 29 April 2015.

17 Inside Missile Defence, Vol. 21 (7), 1 April 2015.

18 The GBI, comprising of a booster vehicle and an Exo-atmospheric Kill-Vehicle (EKV), flies to a projected intercept point upon threat identification. The EKV uses its in-built propulsion and guidance control for final-seconds decisions to acquire the target, perform identification and steer itself to the warhead. See "Testing: Building Confidence," *BMD Fact Book*, Missile Defence Agency, 2009.

repeated developmental test failures, the project had seen multiple revivals after successful interceptions in 2006 and 2014. After initial deployment in Alaska and California, the plan was to deploy over 30 GBIs by 2010, and raise it to over 44 by 2013, though this got delayed due to these failures. This also affected the initial plan to deploy the GBI as the primary interceptor for the BMD system in Eastern Europe.[19] An upgraded Capability Enhancement-I Exo-Atmospheric Kill Vehicle (EKV) was integrated into the GBI for the 2013 test, which failed to undertake the intercept. A 2nd generation EKV version—the Capability Enhancement-II—was successfully flight-tested in the summer of 2014.[20] Last reported in 2015, the GMDS have cost over $41 billion, with the Missile Defence Agency now reportedly assessing if operational tests till date have developed reliable and effective capabilities under realistic conditions against existing missile threats (referred to as Iran and North Korea, though Russia and China could fall within the ambit).[21]

Currently, the only system that is deemed to have a partial mid-course interception capability is the *Aegis* BMD. Formerly known as the Navy Theatre Wide, the BMD system is integrated on *Aegis* destroyers and forms the foremost sea-based component. The main interceptor is the Standard Missile-3 (SM-3) with over 270 km range and capability to engage short- to interim-range missiles in their late ascent or early descent stage. The *Aegis* system has the dual-functionality of being a first-tier mobile interceptor as well as that of a forward-deployed early-warning system.[22] Known to be currently deployed on over 22 ships, the long-term plan is of

---

19 For a contemporary overview, see http://www.defenceindustrydaily.com/3979m-next-step-or-last-step-for-gmd-05229/, 1 June 2015, accessed March 2016.

20 "First in 6 years: Troubled US missile defence system hits test target," *Russia Today*, 23 June 2014, at https://www.rt.com/usa/167728-gmd-launch-successful-failure/, accessed August 2015.

21 Inside Missile Defence, Vol.21 (14), 8 July 2015.

22 The Aegis System integrates the SPY-1 radar, the MK41 Vertical Launching System and the Long Range Surveillance and Tracking system. Together with the X-band radar, the Aegis can track and engage multiple targets simultaneously.

44 Aegis ships with the SM-3 and -6. The current SM-3 Block I is expected to achieve greater strides towards a mid-course capability, and possibly even a boost-phase, after upgrade to Block IIA, undertaken jointly with Japan. Another version, the Block IIIA, is being developed for the Eastern European system. The successful intercept of a dysfunctional satellite by the SM-3 in February 2008, while demonstrating its ASAT utility, also validated the interceptor's capability to engage targets at a speed of over 22,000 mph. The upgrade to SM-6 is also ongoing, which gives the *Aegis* the status of being the first such system to have ship-based anti-air warfare and anti-ballistic missile operations. In August 2015, the SM-6 Block-I undertook a successful flight test by shooting down an incoming missile. With a budget of $15.3 million, the SM-6 is expected to be the mainstay of the current terminal interception options of the US BMD architecture.[23] Through the Aegis Ashore programme, the sea-based capabilities of Aegis and SM have been transformed into land-based adaptations for the EPAA, and are currently deployed in Romania and Poland. There are demands for a similar deployment of Ashore in Florida for US east coast defence.

Of the boost-phase technologies, the most visible in terms of innovation has been the Airborne Laser (ABL) programme— the world's first high-energy laser weapon on an aerial platform operating inside Earth's atmosphere. The system consisted of a chemical oxygen-iodine laser (COIL) mounted on redesigned Boeing-747 aircraft.[24] The first ABL aircraft rolled out in October 2006, with the laser system undergoing many ground-based tests in the initial years before being integrated on the test aircraft.[25] The fate of the programme was dependent on the laser system's capability to shoot down a boosting missile during flight. In-

---

23 Inside Missile Defence, Vol.21 (15), 27 July 2015.

24 The aircraft crew operates the laser at altitudes of around 40,000 feet, by flying over friendly territory and scanning the horizon for the plumes of rising missiles. For more on the ABL functioning, see A. Vinod Kumar, "Airborne Laser Aircraft Rolls Out," *IDSA Strategic Comments*, 6 November 2006.

25 An in-flight weapon test in August 2009 tested the COIL's intensity through an onboard calorimeter.

Flight testing of the system in 2010 proved the system's ability to track, acquire, and destroy a boosting missile. However, the bulky chemical laser system and an in-flight jitter problem were impediments in the effective operationalisation of this system, along with huge costs. Consequently, the Obama administration confined the ABL programme to a single aircraft in 2010 and eventually scrapped the programme in 2011.[26]

Along with these interception technologies, the US BMD programme also involved a layered sensor network, through ground, sea, and space-based platforms. An array of high-power platforms like the sea-based X-Band radar, Upgraded Early Warning Radars (UEWRs) in California and UK, a Cobra Dane radar in Alaska, and AN/TPY-2 in Japan and Israel, together form overarching battle management, command and control, and surveillance network. The X-Band radar, integrated on a naval platform in 2005, has since been conducting the world's only BMD patrol in conjunction with the AN/TPY-2 sensors. For space-based sensors, NASA has been working on the STSS low-orbit satellites with infrared sensors to track missile launches, midcourse flight and re-entry, and an NFIRE satellite for signature collation assistance. The Space-Based Infrared System (SBIRS), meanwhile, had to be supplanted with the Alternative Infrared Satellite System (AIRSS), due to cost overruns.

(b) Russian BMD Ventures:

The Soviets had the first viable ABM system, the A-35/A-350 (ABM-1), by the 1960s. The ABM-1 consisted of the Galosh three-stage solid-fuelled interceptor missile, which had a range of over 300 km, thus perceivably achieving exo-atmospheric capability as early as 1968.[27] After the ABM treaty, the A-35 was deployed outside Moscow consisting of 64 nuclear-tipped *Galosh*

---

26 Inside Missile Defence, Vol. 21 (7), 19 August 2015.

27 "Strategic Defence and Space Operations," *Soviet Military Power 1987*, at http://www.fas.org/irp/dia/product/smp_87_ch3.htm, accessed October 2009. Also see, "Missile Defence: The First Sixty Years," *Missile Defence Agency Backgrounder*, 15 August 2008, www.mda.mil/mdalink/pdf/first60.pdf, accessed April 2012.

systems. The Soviets upgraded this architecture to ABM-1B and 2 in the 1970s with an upgraded liquid third-stage *Galosh*.[28] This system was to be replaced in 1987 by the A-135 (ABM-3) layered system with endo and exo-atmospheric capabilities, comprising the long-range *Gorgon* (SH-11/ABM-4/51T6), the short-range *Gazelle* (SH-08/ABM-3/53T6), and the *Pillbox* phased-array radar. The *Gorgon* is a 3-stage liquid rocket with 350-km exo-atmospheric range,[29] while the short-range *Gazelle* is a two-stage endo-atmospheric system with 80-km range. Many reports indicate that the Soviet armed forces were not satisfied with the initial performance of the system and sought further improvements with the intended deployment in the mid-1990s. The upgrade of the A-135 was underway with the last test known to be in December 2006.[30] Though developed in the final years of the Cold War as an apparent response to the SDI and coming into operation after the Soviet collapse, standard Russian descriptions about the A-135 talked about pursuing a "modest" capability to intercept nuclear missiles.[31] Whether it was the Cold War years or the first decade of the Russian Federation's strategic posturing, Moscow seemed keen to under-emphasize the potency of its ABM ventures, unlike in the case of offensive forces.

Nonetheless, the post-Soviet Russian BMD architecture has gradually emerged into a vibrant project, in the footsteps of the US programme albeit exhibiting a different character. The primary arm of Russian BMD is its theatre defence platforms which integrate both anti-missile and air defence roles as operationally compatible components in a comprehensive architecture. The

---

28 The ABM-2 consisted of the S-225 endo-atmospheric interceptor developed during the early 1970s; see www.fas.org/spp/starwars/program/soviet/s-225.htm.

29 Over 32 *Gorgons* and over 68 *Gazelles* are currently deployed around Moscow. For more details on the System A-135, see www.missilethreat.com/missiledefencesystems/id.7/system_detail.asp.

30 "Russia conducts test of missile defence system," 5 December 2006, http://en.rian.ru/russia/20061205/56477126.html, accessed October 2015.

31 "Very modest expectations: performance of Moscow missile defence," 2012, at: http://russianforces.org/blog/2012/10/very_modest_expectations_sovie.shtml, accessed October 2015.

core of Russia's theatre defence forays includes the S-300, S-400, and the futuristic S-500 programmes. The S-300 is developed in two variants: the S-300P (SA-10/PMU *Grumble*) and the S-300V (SA-12A *Gladiator*, SA-12B *Giant*).[32] The S-400 (SA-20 *Triumf*), Russia's relatively latest show-piece air defence system with ABM capability, is an upgrade of the S-300, with an extended coverage range of over 400km range and interception altitude of 30 km.[33] The system is envisioned for both augmented air defence as well as BMD roles with its capability to target short- and medium-range missiles, aircraft, and other aerodynamic threats with effective ranges up to 2200 miles.[34] The S-500 is the ambitious project planned to match the US mid-course interceptors with an intended exo-atmospheric range of 3,500 km.

In the post-S-400 phase, officials propound that Russia would be working on compact and manoeuvrable fifth-generation air defence/ABM systems which "combine the elements of air, missile and space defence for targeting enemy system deeper into space"—implying an intention to gain greater exo-atmospheric capabilities.[35] The long-term goal will be to provide a lethal mix to the offensive and defensive capabilities of the Russian Strategic Forces, with the twin strategies of (a) overwhelming US BMD deployment in Eastern Europe and Asia through

---

32 The S-300P system is designed to detect, track, and destroy incoming ballistic missiles, cruise missiles, and low-flying aircraft. The S-300P has been modified several times, the recent variants being the S-300PMU-1 (SA-10D) and the S-300PMU-2 (SA-10E Favorit).

33 The S-400 consists of an upgraded S-300 missile, multi-target radar, and observation and tracking vehicles which can simultaneously track and guide missiles to multiple targets. For more on the S-400 see, www.missilethreat.com/missiledefencesystems/id.52/ system_detail.asp, accessed March 2009.

34 On 6 August 2007, Russia deployed the S-400 *Triumf* air defence system in Elektrostal, outside Moscow. See also, "Russia unveils air defence, eyes U.S. missile shield," 6 August, 2007, at: http://in.reuters.com/article/worldNews/idINIndia-28848420070806?sp=true, accessed March 2009.

35 "Russia working on missile to hit targets in space," Statement by Russian Air Force Commander, Colonel General Alexander Zelin, *The Times of India*, 9 August 2007.

systems like Topol-M (SS-25/27)[36] and the hypersonic Yu-71,[37] and (b) challenge the US offence capability through advanced interception systems, chiefly at the terminal and mid-course stages. The dramatic shift in Russian posturing came in March 2018 when President Vladimir Putin announced a series of new generation (nuclear-armed and nuclear-powered) weapon systems claiming to have capabilities of global reach, the ability to negate BMD systems and the firepower to trigger a nuclear catastrophe. Fundamentally aimed at defeating the US missile defences, the new offensive inventory has the potential to be a game-changer for global nuclear dynamics and the deterrence structures between the great powers (details in Preface).

(c) Other BMD pursuits:

Though many countries are pursuing interception technologies of various genres, only a handful could make notable inroads in this arena. Israel, for example, has the most vibrant missile defence architecture, with a plethora of systems that stand out for their targeting innovations and range of capabilities. Israel's multi-layered architecture comprises of systems that could intercept the shortest-range of rockets as well as the longer range systems that could provide interception against strategic missiles.[38] The *Iron Dome*, for example, is a frontline system targeting short-range or shoulder-launched rockets fired by militant groups, and with the capability to accurately track and intercept multiple incoming projectiles in rapid succession. The medium-range system in Israeli armoury is *David's Sling* (Magic Wand), which

---

36 At a speed of 10,000 km/hr, the Topol-M is supposed to the fastest ICBM, with the capability for mid-flight manoeuvre.

37 Kukil Bora,"Russia's Secret Hypersonic Nuclear Missile Yu-71 Can Breach Existing Missile Defence Systems: Experts," *Ibtimes*, 29 June 2015, at http://www.ibtimes.com/russias-secret-hypersonic-nuclear-missile-yu-71-can-breach-existing-missile-defence-1987590.

38 For an overview of Israeli interception capability, see http://www.jewishvirtuallibrary.org/jsource/talking/88_missiledefence.html, accessed August 2015.

could intercept missiles with a range of over 300 km.[39] Mainly intended for missile threats from Lebanon and Syria, the David's Sling has the *Stunner* interceptor, which is jointly developed by Israel's Missile Defence Organisation and the US MDA. The longer-range interceptor deployed by Israel is the Arrow-2 (and 3), also jointly developed with the MDA, and is intended as a strategic defence against Iranian missiles (including nuclear-tipped systems). Besides this array, Israel has developed a series of advanced interceptor systems, namely the *Spyder, Hawk, Shavit,* and *Nimrod*—all with varying augmented air defence capabilities, besides co-producing a Long Range Surface-to-Air Missile (LRSAM) with Indian companies and defence forces.[40]

China and India are the other major players which are competing to make advances in this domain. After publicly opposing missile defences for many years by highlighting their potential to weaponise outer space, China made a dramatic entry into a strategic interception with an Anti-Satellite (ASAT) test in 2007, followed by a ballistic missile interception in 2010, and a supposedly endo-atmospheric interception test in 2013, and a mid-course interception in 2018. Like Israel, China is also known to be developing strategic air defence systems with missile defence capabilities. The known Chinese projects include the FT-2000 and variants of the *Hongqi* system (*Hongqi*-2, 9, 10 & 15), assumed to be based on Russian systems like the S-75 and S-300 PMU. Propelled by the HQ-9 and HQ-15 missiles, the FT-2000 is intended to achieve interception coverage of over 150-200 km. (The Indian and Chinese ventures are covered in detail in the subsequent chapters). However, unlike the Israeli advances, the projects pursued by India and China are still in various stages of development and may take some more years to see actual deployment.

---

39 "Israel test-fires "David's Sling" missile defence system," *Russia Today*, 2 April 2015, at https://www.rt.com/news/246093-israel-tests-david-sling/, accessed October 2015.

40 Israel has also developed a short-range interceptor called the "Iron Dome", and a medium-range interceptor called "Magic Wand". See, *www.israeli-weapons.com/israeli_weapons_missile_systems.html*, accessedSeptember 2016.

Where is the technology headed for?

This being the overall development picture of these baseline technologies, it is pertinent to examine how many of these technologies could progress towards deployment, and what the technological map of this domain will look like in the coming future. It will be useful to know the direction in which the nuclear environment will be transforming if it is at all impacted by the permeation of BMD technology. However, forecasting the probable/possible direction of BMD technology is always a difficult endeavour. The longer the period of forecast, greater will be the challenges to predict in a near-precise manner. Technology futures and their modelling have often been pursued through imaginative narratives, taking the shape of science fiction, alongside rigorous scientific methods.[41] Various tools, including methods like Delphi (tacit knowledge), analogy (study of another comparable system), extrapolation (observation from the sample system), statistics (based on variables to be predicted) and causal relations (studying the phenomenon), have been used for futures research, along with analytical methods like genius forecasting, simulations, scenario building, cross-impact matrix, decision trees, etc.[42] Though these methods have inherent limitations, adapting suitable models for specific cases or an assortment of methodologies can assist forecasts. For example, the usage of comparatively easier denominators like the natural identification of a system/technology's evolution and progression route in the probable/possible "life curve" of a concept, or the "road mapping" of this evolution, can help in forecasting the structural progress of technologies. Often, the key to such approaches lies in *identifying the trends, mapping the possible/probable innovations*, and *imagining revolutions* of a technological construct.

---

41 Some of the noted works include: Nikita Lary and Bertrand de Jouvenel, *The Art of Conjecture*, New York: Basic Books, 1967; S. Makridakis, "The Art and Science of Forecasting," *International Journal of Forecasting*, Vol. 2, 1986; T. Modis, *Predictions: Society's Telltale Signature Reveals the Past and Forecasts the Future*, New York: Simon& Schuster, 1992; M. Dublin, *Futurehype: The Tyranny of Prophecy*, Plume: New York, 1989.

42 David S. Walonick, "An overview of forecasting methodology," 1993, at: www.satpac.com/research-papers/forecasting.htm, accessed August 2009.

Like many military technologies, the development cycles of missile defence technologies have spanned a 10–20 year period. Hence, one could start with the assumption that most technological paradigms (or concepts) in BMD development are readily existent, and are not expected to dramatically alter in the next two decades, but for a few systems. The probable/possible route of the technological development process currently underway could, however, be influenced by the innovations in existing technological paradigms. As a causal relationship variable, strong political drivers could shape the progress of these development processes or radically change their character, as is seen in the US BMD programmes and how others have responded to it. However, this evolution could also move in a *ceteris paribus* (where all other factors remain constant) condition, implying that technological lifecycles would move in predictable phases of conceptualization, development, maturity, and consolidation before eventual deployment, and that political drivers might not dramatically transform the nature of technological concepts, if not the developmental process as such, in a given period of time. However, considering that political drivers are too potent a variable to be overlooked in the military-technological realm, its causal impact could be inducted at appropriate levels of analysis in order to infer the possible shifts in the development life-cycles or influences on the conceptualisation processes itself.

For example, in the American programmes, various development periods like C1, C2 and C3 of the Strategic Defence Initiative Organisation (SDIO) phase or Block I, II and III of the Missile Defence Agency (MDA) phase, carried a 5–10 year development period from conceptualization to development maturity of technology baselines. Yet, most of the matured technologies took an average of 10–15 years to complete the development life-cycle before moving into deployment phases. While technological templates remained constant during this period, the nature of decisions on conceptualisation or development was influenced by political drivers, including the change in the strategic environment and the influence of political leadership or ideologies. The US BMD development since SDI years embodies this phenomenon. While the Cold War dynamics influenced the nature of SDI-era technologies like *Brilliant Pebbles* and directed energy programmes, the end of the Cold War and change in dispensations affected only the development programmes—and not the technological concepts, many of which continued to be pursued through new nomenclatures. Though political factors—like the ABM Treaty—affected the development of space-based interceptors, the concept remained prevalent as the US continued to vouch for the military uses of space platforms. Incidentally, the ABM Treaty, despite being a major political driver, could only block the deployment of BMD systems, but not the research and development in this domain.

Assuming that the MDA would take another 10-15 years to realistically deploy its comprehensive nationwide layered defence based on existing technological concepts, the space for the next 15 years or so could also involve the development of new concepts. Here, the key variable could be the political drivers that might influence this process. Even as imaginative thinking could hold roost, technological predictions of a 15–20 year period would be as challenging as forecasting the political spectrum. Nonetheless, going by the evolution of BMDs since the 1950s, the nature of technological progress of such a timeframe could very much be within the limits of realistic imagination. As some programmes given below would testify, technologies thought about in the 1960s are being revived for future development, with deployment plans of 10–15 years from now. Many components of SDI when initially conceptualized were then thought to be in the realms of science fiction, but have since been pursued and achieved, though in limited terms. In fact, a closer look at the ABL and *Aegis* SM-3/6 projects will show their lineage to the US Air Force's Airborne Ballistic Missile Intercept System (ABMIS), and the US Navy's Sea-Based Anti-Ballistic Missile Intercept System (SABMIS).[43]

Some of the contemporary baseline technologies have immense potential to emerge as futuristic applications owing to their innovative characteristics and creative magnificence. They

---

43 "Missile Defence: The First Sixty Years," n.27.

include concepts like Airborne Laser (ABL), Kinetic Energy Interceptor (KEI), and *Brilliant Pebbles*, among others. These technologies cover a whole spectrum of directed and kinetic energy concepts as well as space-based applications that could bring revolutionary changes to military strategies. The concept of hitting a ground-based or flying target from an aerial platform through a laser beam is undoubtedly a futuristic technology, which cannot be overlooked, especially because much headway has been achieved by the MDA. Going by the progress made on the ABL, there are seemingly only a few technical challenges that constrain this programme from fruition, the significant one being the capability to focus a high-powered beam on a rapidly-moving target while maintaining intensity amid atmospheric absorption and aircraft-centric jitters before going for the kill.[44]

In fact, the current development plan of the MDA is precisely focussed on reviving various directed energy programmes, primarily the laser systems. A plethora of laser kill vehicles are currently under development and destined for various services. Of all, the ABL has seen a reincarnation through a smaller and lighter laser weapon system to be integrated on to a tactical aircraft, namely the AC-130, with a demonstration plan for 2017–18, and potential fielding by 2020. Similarly, the High Energy Liquid Laser Area Defence System (HELLADS) is a venture to develop a 150 kw laser weapon system that will be ten times smaller and lighter than current lasers of similar power, enabling integration on tactical aircraft to defend against ground threats. The focus is to have "simultaneous power and beam capability," attain success at "30 kw and less", and design "several viable laser architectures."[45] The shift is not just towards smaller and lighter laser systems, but also to move from chemical to solid-state and electric lasers.

---

44 In July 2007, the MDA tested the ABL's ability to target a missile with tracking beams, to adjust for atmospheric disturbances and to start the high-powered destructor laser sequence. See,*Global Security Newswire*, 31 July 2007, at www.nti.org/d_ newswire/issues/2007_7_31.html#C2278269, accessed September 2009.

45 Inside Missile Defence, Vol.21 (17), 19 August 2015.

Following up on this momentum, various wings of the US defence forces have been seeking a new directed energy development roadmap to build customised laser systems for their operations. Boeing has been working with the US Army to create the High Energy Laser Mobile Demonstrator (HELMD)—a compact laser weapon system with 2 kw laser and 10–15 second kill duration—as a mobile system to target Combat-Unmanned Aerial Vehicles (C-UAVs). Other improvisations that are being pursued include lasers with 50-60 kw, and kill within 2–3 seconds of launch. The US Navy, for its part, is working on the Naval Laser Weapon System (LaWS), while the US Air Force has the SHIELD programme, which will be a solid-state 10 kw high-energy laser weapon that will be integrated into a pod and installed in fighter aircraft by 2020. Adding fillip to these initiatives is the proposal to develop a series of terminal/boost-phase interception systems, especially exploring the scope of installing smaller laser systems on combat-UAVs which could fly at high altitudes.[46] Estimating to cost over US$ 30 million, the long-endurance UAVs flying above the clouds, into the stratosphere, could aim at the ambitious task of undertaking boost-phase interception within 1–5 minutes of the enemy missile launch. The Global Hawk, which could fly at 60,000 feet, is considered for this venture with the integration of a 50 kw combined fibre laser system. However, the possibility of being vulnerable to enemy air defences while operating in close proximity of the target is cited as a certain drawback for such programmes, though a C-UAV is not seen as a highly valuable asset to be compromised in a strategic condition.

A challenging area for research and development since the 1950s has been the development of requisite kill-vehicle technologies. While nuclear and explosive payloads were initially in use, the concept of a kinetic kill vehicle (KKV) has been in vogue since the SDI days. Many of the current systems, including the GBI, SM-3, and ABM-3 (even THAAD, when interception is beyond atmosphere) use exo-atmospheric hit-to-kill vehicle (EKV). Unlike directed energy, KKVs are deemed to be more cost-effective as their power is dependent on the interceptor velocity

---

46 Inside Missile Defence, Vol.21 (5), 4 March 2015.

and mass of the payload. Yet, some KKV projects, like the Kinetic Energy Interceptor (KEI), had not found much favour, probably owing to similarities with GBI which had its own developmental struggles. The KEI was supposed to be a high-energy, 3-stage interceptor which could travel at 12,000 mph, and was meant to target medium, interim-range, and ICBMs in boost and midcourse phases.[47] Highly mobile and transportable in a C-135, the KEI launcher deployment comes with many choices of either proximity deployment to the launch site of the enemy missile or as a mid-course interceptor. Though the KEI was considered as a replacement for the SM-3 in *Aegis*, its weight and size limitations for the Aegis (VLS) launchers, besides its huge costs, led to its rejection. However, the concept of advanced KKVs remains strong, as is evident from the revival of the Advanced Technology Kill Vehicle (ATKV) of SDI days. The ATKV, known to be considered for SM-3 Block IIA, was expected to significantly improve the missile's acceleration and final velocity due to its lightweight, and provide a better suite of sensors than the EKV.

The programme has now been improvised into the Multiple Object Kill Vehicles (MOKV) project—placing a number of KVs on a single warhead to simultaneously engage several targets. The MOKV is the 2nd phase of the Common Kill Vehicle Technology Programme, which will develop a re-designed kill vehicle for the GBI. An earlier version—the Multiple Kill Vehicle (MKV)— was terminated in 2009 despite proving capability to "hover on own power and track surrogate targets", but had serious other technical challenges. The revamped MOKV will seek to destroy several objects within a threat complex by considering advanced sensor, divert, and altitude command and control concepts."[48] As a result, exo-atmospheric kills of the future would involve multiple (independently operating) kill-vehicles from a single interceptor that could be effective against MIRV threats as well

---

47 The system had a successful flight test in September 2006, and was destined to replace the SM-3 in the Aegis ships. For more on the KEI, see www. military.com/soldiertech/0,14632,Soldiertech_KEI,,00.html, accessed September 2009.

48 Inside Missile Defence, Vol.21 (17), 19 August 2015.

as countermeasures. The MDA has contracted US\$ 9 million to Raytheon and Lockheed Martin to develop a prototype of MOKV by 2022.

On the other hand, the spectrum which remains largely out-of-bounds for missile defence experimentations is the space frontier, owing to the global consensus against the militarization of space, and legal covenants like the United Nations Outer Space Treaty and PAROS,[49] though countries like the USA are favouring military uses of outer space, if not actual weaponisation. Even during the Cold War, the ABM Treaty largely restricted programmes like *Brilliant Pebbles*, as a result of which the space frontier was confined to surveillance, early warning sensors, and tracking applications. While these applications would continue in the coming decades, there is pressure from sections in the US scientific and military establishment to optimally exploit outer-space for missile defence applications.[50]

In fact, an independent group recommended the revival of space-based interceptors of SDI-era for a layered interception, along with a space test-bed.[51] Though an outright revival is unlikely, the fear of rising ASAT capabilities among nations like China, the enduring challenge from long-range missile proliferation, slow progress in ground-based technologies, etc., could contribute to at least some capabilities of interception being considered for space-

---

49 The United Nations Outer Space Treaty provides the basic framework on international space law affirming that space should be reserved for peaceful uses. It came into effect in October 1967. Towards the end of 2000, the UN General Assembly had voted on a resolution called the "Prevention of Outer Space Arms Race." In October 2006, 166 nations voted for a resolution to prevent an arms race in outer space. While Israel abstained, the USA voted against.

50 Besides the Pentagon request for a billion dollars space-based weapon programmes in 2008, the US Joint Chiefs of Staff urge "full spectrum dominance" in space while the 2006 National Space Policy explains that the USA will "preserve its rights, capabilities, and freedom of action in space; dissuade others from either impeding those rights; take those actions necessary to protect its space capabilities; and deny, if necessary, adversaries the use of space capabilities hostile to US national interests."

51 "Missile Defence, Space Relationship, and the Twenty First Century," n.27.

based deployment. That Russia is also seeking to exploit outer-space resources in a formidable manner also reflects the renewed interest in exploiting this domain. As a result, a host of advanced tracking and sensor technologies is likely to be developed, especially in the low-earth orbit, with high-resolution tracking capabilities to assist key applications in boost and a midcourse interception, even as deeper space endeavours might follow suit in future.

Besides these, a host of other critical projects are now at the conceptualization stage at the MDA. They include advancements in surveillance and early-warning domains, namely the Early Launch Detection and Tracking (ELDT) system, which is meant to cover tracking gaps in the initial launch seconds, and the Over-the-Horizon Radar (OTHR) which could pick up signals over longer ranges for early launch detection.[52] Another interesting concept with shades of the ABL, minus the kill-medium, is the High-Altitude Airship (HAA)—an unmanned air-ship to carry sensors and tracking systems over hostile areas to detect and monitor launch possibilities. Then, there is *Project Hercules* which also intends to develop robust detection, tracking, and discrimination algorithms, to help in faster identification and targeting. Similarly, a technology called MEMS (microminiaturized electro-mechanical systems) is being developed to assist the MKV goals.

On the other hand, one major manifestation of the advent of futuristic concepts in ongoing technology planning and development trends is the not-so-subtle invocation of cyberspace. The MDA managers are increasingly talking about the "use of cyber means to neutralize enemy missiles short of shooting mid-flight." This marks a significant paradigm shift in terms of doctrinal orientation for BMD programmes.[53] This entails the use of virtual attacks on missile-relevant targets that could redress many of the problems that are recurrent with traditional missile defence systems. MDA planners term this as a "Left-of-Launch"

---

52 Gary Payton, "Advanced Concepts in Missile Defence", *Washington Roundtable on Science and Public Affairs*, George C. Marshall Institute, Washington, 12 September 2005.

53 Inside Missile Defence, Vol.21 (14), 8 July 2015.

approach, which implies pre-emptive cyber attacks on enemy facilities to prevent launch/firing (squashing release while still on the ground).[54] Cyber forms the core of the left-of-launch approach which, along with non-kinetic options, could mainstream "passive and non-offensive postures" as the core character of US missile defence strategy.

There are two aspects about these development trends and futuristic concepts that need emphasis. First, the USA remains the technology leader in this domain, with the most advanced interceptor concepts being developed in its programmes. After the Cold War, Russia did not derive the capability to invest heavily in advanced technologies and hence, initially, opted for cheaper theatre and air defence systems before reviving tit-for-tat capabilities that could match the US programmes. But for Russia, Israel and Japan, most other military powers are still working on rudimentary BMD technologies. Second, it is clear that the future course of BMD technology development will invariably be determined by political drivers. While missile and WMD proliferation scenarios will remain a constant factor, political conditioning, especially in Washington, will drastically decide the fate of these concepts and the course of innovations. Though BMD technologies will endure and might even trigger a new arms race, the momentum for disarmament could drastically affect the innovation pace.

However, the brighter side for the field would be the radical augmentations in theatre and augmented air defences which, in all likelihood, would thrive due to their tactical nature and cost-effectiveness. Driven by newer, lower-tier threats, especially from non-state actors, a new generation of advanced air defence systems, with capabilities for point and area defence, is on the ascendancy. A handful of these systems are currently in operation and stand out for their technological brilliance, the noteworthy ones being the *Sky Shield* and the *Skyguard* systems. The *Sky*

---

54 See "Left of Launch," 16 March 2015, http://missiledefenseadvocacy.org/ alert/3132/, accessed October 2017. Also see, William J. Broad and David E. Sanger, "US Strategy to Hobble North Korea was Hidden in Plain Sight," *New York Times*, 4 March 2017.

Shield 35 uses a unique 35-mm AHEAD (Advanced Hit Efficiency and Destruction) shell that ejects sub-projectiles on the path of the incoming target, especially aircraft and short-range missiles. Derived from the Tactical High Energy Laser programme (THEL), the *Skyguard* (*Nautilus*) is an air defence system that uses *laser cannons to create a protective shield* of over 10 km radius over strategic zones like airports, urban areas, or force deployments to protect against short-range threats.[55] Another system of this variety is the *HAWK* Air Defence[56]—supposedly the world's most advanced all-weather, medium-altitude air defence system in service since the 1960s. There are other prominent ones of this genre, like the MBDA's *Aster SAMP/T*—a limited-TMD system designed to provide point/area defence against lower-tier threats, and *Spada* 2000—an all-weather air defence system with a range of up to 60km, and capable of intercepting targets at 25 km while engaging four simultaneously. For that matter, innovation will not elude the lower tier as well in this evolution!

---

55 A product of U.S.-Israel cooperation, the THEL was conceptualised to deal with the short-range rocket menace from Hezbollah. In July 2006, Northrop Grumman unveiled the *Skyguard* system; see www.gizmag.com/go/5868/, accessed September 2009.

56 The development details of the current upgrade, the Phase III HAWK, can be accessed at *www.raytheon.com/products/hawk/*, accessed November 2017.

CHAPTER III

MISSILE DEFENCE AND NUCLEAR DETERRENCE

Since the dawn of the nuclear age, nuclear deterrence has emerged, evolved and survived in the shadow of defensive capabilities like ABM systems. These systems, ironically, were embargoed out from strategic and operational domains owing to their destabilising factor, though the development of the technology and pursuit of the capability continued to influence the deterrence calculus between the superpowers. Deterrence, in the manner it existed between the superpowers during the Cold War, and followed subsequently as a template by other nuclear powers, worked on the basis of a reasonable arrangement: there could be a formidable presence (and even a balance) of strategic forces which could *survive a pre-emptive nuclear attack* or *a first strike* and would *launch a massive retaliation* that could *inflict unacceptable damage* on the adversary.[1] Accordingly, it was premised that: (a) the costs of attacking a state would outweigh the adversary's perceived benefits, (b) the nuclear-armed state could convey a capability and intention to retaliate to an attack in order for the threat of assured destruction or unacceptable damage to be credible, and dissuade the adversary, (c) the adversary should

---

1   Among the many definitions, one such classical elucidation was to define deterrence as a state's assured destruction capability that gives it the ability to make the cost that an adversary has to bear in any conflict outweigh any potential gains. See Robert Powell, "Nuclear Deterrence Theory, Nuclear Proliferation and National Missile Defence," *International Security*, 27(4), Spring 2003.

be a rational actor who is convinced about the costs and gains of initiating an attack.

Nuclear-armed states were, thus, destined to operate in an environment of mutually assured destruction, with the fear of certain retaliation and unacceptable damage deterring each other from initiating a nuclear conflict. As policymakers and deterrence theorists tried to perfect this logic, questions remained on how stability could be assured in a volatile environment that is gripped by suspicion, mistrust, and the potential for miscommunication.[2] Also, concerns were evoked on how much "unacceptable" damage could be guaranteed, the fear of which could deter the adversary from taking the first plunge, and whether forces will survive sufficiently to endow a massive retaliation.

In fact, the two elements that needed to be maintained for this equation to work was the guaranteed *survivability* of retaliatory forces, and the circumstantial environment to ensure that retaliation will not be *negated* or *defended* upon by the adversary through defensive systems like ballistic missile defence. It is peculiar that survivability was a psychological belief of nuclear powers prodded by their faithful investments in "seemingly secure" deep-earth silos (and mobile naval platforms), assuming impregnability from or limited vulnerability to a nuclear first strike. On the other hand, the headway made by the Soviet Union and the USA in

---

2   A wave of analyses came through the development of the nuclear deterrence theory which was subsequently perfected into policy by statesmen like Robert McNamara. Early contributions to the deterrence theory included Bernard Brodie, *Strategy in the Missile Age*, Princeton University Press, Princeton, N.J., 1959; Albert Wohlstetter, "The Delicate balance of Terror," *Foreign Affairs*, 37(2), January 1959; Herman Kahn, *On Thermonuclear War*, Princeton: Princeton University Press, 1960; Thomas C. Shelling, *The Strategy of Conflict*, Cambridge: Harvard University Press, 1960; Glenn H. Snyder, *Deterrence and Defence*, Princeton: Princeton University Press, 1966, among others. Deterrence theory witnessed substantive discourses that facilitated new thinking, like the Rational Deterrence Theory (RDT). Notable ones include Robert Jervis, "Deterrence Theory Revisited," *World Politics*, 31, January 1979; Christopher H. Achen and Duncan Snidal, "Rational Deterrence Theory and Comparative Case Studies," *World Politics*, 41, January 1989; Robert Jervis, "Rational Deterrence: Theory and Evidence," *World Politics*, 41(2), January 1989, among others.

the development of interception technologies seemed to unsettle the scope for mutual vulnerability and diminish the tenability of deterrence. That they agreed on the ABM Treaty to maintain inviolability of mutual vulnerability was a creative contribution to deterrence stability, howsoever notional.

Why then did both nations continue to pursue ABM technologies which could vitiate this notion of stability? There are some normative and psychological factors that could have prodded the trend. First, deterrence, by and large, was a means to propagate stability, but that hardly mattered in eliminating political conflicts or in redressing the recurring security dilemmas, a phenomenon termed by Robert Powell as a "fundamental credibility problem" of deterrence.[3] Second, notwithstanding the perceptions of existential deterrence and retaliatory capabilities, keeping vulnerabilities open never evoked confidence for both parties, with a high trust deficit defining their competitive relationship.[4] The third could be the twin problem of the survivability of second-strike forces, and the implications if and when a vulnerability is exploited. For, even the possibility of a single nuclear missile pouncing upon any of the other was sufficient trigger for a full-fledged nuclear war in an equation where both nations maintained hair-trigger alerts. Despite the best of measures, both countries were unsure whether their leadership or forces might survive to undertake retaliation which, even if initiated, might only complement the catastrophe, not the winnability. The fourth factor flowing out of these apprehensions highlights the fact that nuclear deterrence operated in a condition of self-doubt, with the fear of annihilation, misperceptions, and accidental wars remaining a constant.

Even deterrence theorists have never shied away from doubting the durability of deterrence. In Brodie's words, "deterrence must thus remain effective although it has no chance to prove its efficacy in practice. The automaticity of retaliation

---

3   See Powell, n.1.

4   Though mistrust was a standard feature of great power relations during the Cold War, an interesting instance to note are the tussles seen during the nuclear test ban negotiations in the early 1960s.

is taken too much for granted."[5] In fact, the influence of self-deterrence has been cited as a hindrance in perfecting the nuclear deterrence theory. That countries operate in a psychological environment of varying confidence levels reflects strongly on deterrence postures. For, despite threats of massive retaliation and assured destruction or beaming confidence about survivable second-strike capabilities, the element of self-doubt about national survival and fear of annihilation underlines the behaviour and psychology of deterrence postures. No wonder then, despite the reassurance of the ABM Treaty, the superpowers did not fail to realize the improprieties of keeping vulnerabilities open.

The development tracks of ABM/BMD technology since 1972 indicate how, in spite of the ABM Treaty, both nations continued with the pursuit of not merely advanced interceptors but also the means to greater accuracy and precision targeting through technologies like directed energy. An alternative approach to the deterrence matrix could be raised to explain this trend: will the threat of massive retaliation or assured destruction be credible deterrence if the state cannot *defend* itself or rather *protect* (its counter-forces and population centres) from a first strike or pre-emptive strike?[6] Further, was reliability on vulnerability a tenable option when the credibility of retaliation was not assured? Why were missile defences not treated as maximizing deterrence if a state's counter-force and counter-value assets could be protected by a defensive shield? The basis of assured destruction was the pre-supposed *survivability* of second-strike forces, predicated on the thinking that though the targeted state could be vulnerable to a first strike, it could *sufficiently protect* its retaliatory capabilities in order to execute a destructive response. In fact, the superpowers were not in denial of the potential of ABM systems to provide comprehensive protection to second strike assets as well as population centres. This is best evident in the ABM Treaty's provisions to allow limited ABM coverage over two installations:

---

5   See Brodie, n.2.

6   Some analysts argued that unless the US retains some ability to protect itself, its threats will lack credibility. See Albert Wohlstetter, "Swords without Shields," *National Interest*, No. 8, Summer 1987.

one missile site and one population centre, which was later restricted to one through a mutually-agreed protocol. While the Soviets retained the *Galosh* system over Moscow, their major population centre, the Americans retained their *Safeguard* system in Grand Forks, their key ICBM site.

Strange considerations might emerge from these permutations preferred by the superpowers. Yet, their mutual reluctance to take into consideration the aggregated deterrence utility of ABM systems and, instead, give sacrosanctity to mutual vulnerability seemed to be based on the prevalent thinking of (or rather, a mutual inclination towards) deterrence stability. First, the Americans had sufficiently convinced the Soviets that having a nation-wide defensive capability will create perceptions of defensive depth that will tempt them to attack and annihilate the other.[7] Second, interception technology was then at such a nascent stage of development that it provided little assurance to either party of a credible defensive capability. Third, it was widely feared that the influx of defensive forces will be countered by a massive increase in offensive forces, which could aggravate security dilemmas and arms competitions of the day. Finally, the reliance on defensive systems was not considered constructive to the ongoing dialogue for limiting offensive weapons. As this volume will subsequently highlight in coming chapters, two key utilities of ABM systems— their ability to advance comprehensive defence, and be a guarantor of stability when nuclear powers pursue offensive arms limitations or numerical reductions—were not sufficiently considered, or were rejected during this dialogue phase in the 1960s.

Rationale and Implications of Missile Defence

How much has the scenario changed since the Cold War era that warrants the development and permeation of missile defences today? Is it time to endorse the end of MAD, rather its diminishing utility as a deterrence framework? Or, can it be refined? How will

---

7   There are descriptions on how the Soviets were made to believe about the destabilizing character of defences. Barry Blechman and Jonas Vaicikonis, "Unblocking the road to zero: US-Russian cooperation on missile defences," *Bulletin of the Atomic Scientists*, 66(6), 2010.

nuclear stability be affected or managed if BMD systems begin to complement the deterrence calculus by adding up with the projected strength of the offensive forces?

At the heart of the current strategic transformation denoted by the advent of missile defences will not just be a changed security environment but also the potential initiation of an evolutionary next stage in deterrence dynamics. The paradigmatic shifts in the evolution is a continuum from the Cold War period owing to insufficient redressal by existing structures of enduring issues like deterrence instability and recurring strategic competitions. The continual development of missile defence technology and policy manoeuvering on their deployment might also have influenced these dynamics. There are a handful of areas where this can be explained. First, as argued earlier, leaving vulnerability open has been of no reassurance to the nuclear weapon states. At no point had any of them felt any safer by the prevalence of vulnerability, howsoever mutual. Offensive forces, by their inherent task of providing for an onslaught (whether for pre-emption, attack or for retaliation), were ordained to be creating deterrence in the minds of adversaries. However, issues of survivability and unacceptable destructibility always sustained the imperative of having defences, if and when deterrence was not effective or might fall short. Thus, the reliance on vulnerability-oriented deterrence seemed an imprudent strategy, notwithstanding the fact that it was uniformly shared.

Second, the validity of deterrence as a one-bill-fits-all solution was always susceptible to challenge. It was presupposed that a deterrence equation between the superpowers could be a template for all the theatres where two nuclear powers competed. For example, massive retaliation was customarily applied by the USA as a standard posture against the Soviet Union as well as China, notwithstanding the fact that the latter had a no-first-use doctrine, a qualitative deterrent strategy, and belief in existential deterrence. That Washington had threatened a first strike against China at the peak of a conventional conflict also shows how deterrence infirmities were dominant. Another example is the deterrence imbalance in the South Asian deterrence matrix where one actor's (India) no-first-use posture is disproportionately countered by the other (Pakistan) through an ambiguous posture of potential first-use driven by ill-defined redlines and brinkmanship behaviour leading to recurring crises. The introduction of tactical nuclear weapons in this theatre has also complicated the dominant notions of the second strike. India's signalling that a first-use or first strike, even if it involves tactical weapons, will be responded to with massive retaliation has been perceived in some quarters as confusing, perfunctory, and even prone to escalation. Then, there is the situation in the Korean peninsula where a nuclear-armed despot, Kim Jong-Un of Democratic Peoples' Republic of North Korea (DPRK), had complicated deterrence equations by refusing to be cowed down by threats of either a pre-emptive first strike by his nuclear adversaries or a massive retaliation to a potential nuclear attack which he repeatedly threatens to resort to in the event of military hostilities.[8]

Third, the projection of massive retaliation and catastrophic destruction as outcomes compounded trepidation and resultant security dilemmas that were causal in the revival of the nuclear arms races. This further complicated the deterrence calculus, especially since existential deterrence perceptions of new weapons states did not match the classical benchmarks and drove their quest for capability and technology deeper. That nuclear states, existing and newer, were veering towards quantitative deterrence was not seen as favourable for strategic stability and, instead, gravely drove greater competition.

The fourth factor flows from this complexity—that deterrence cannot mitigate proliferation. Realist arguments influenced nuclear politics by propagating formulations like "the more the better", prompting aspirants to conceive nuclear weapons as the currency of power and survival. Fifth, the continuing pursuit of advanced interception technologies in spite of the ABM Treaty, especially the SDI projects, convinced nuclear powers that the

---

8 For a discussion, see A. Vinod Kumar, "Is the DPRK's Nuclear March Unstoppable?" *BASIC*, 7 November 2017, available at: http://www.basicint. org/blogs/vinod-kumar/11/2017/dprks-nuclear-march-unstoppable, accessed November 2017.

advanced among them will acquire the capability at the first opportunity. Lastly, extended deterrence was not an arrangement that could sustain on mutual vulnerability. Despite US assurances about massive retaliation, Europe was always the frontline that was to incur the toll of a Soviet attack. The need to defend Europe, thus, always remained a standing rationale to construct defences.

If these many factors continue to weigh strongly to justify the relevance of missile defence, the post-Cold War security environment also threw up complexities of deterrence stability that needed to be addressed. In fact, the meaning of strategic stability today is significantly different from what it was during the early Cold War.[9] There are new drivers that complicate equations. First, proliferation dynamics have dramatically changed, with new nuclear weapon states emerging since the end of the Cold War, and newer aspirants preparing to cross the threshold. That newer actors have come at a time when nations are more oriented towards disarmament measures and reducing the salience of nuclear weapons has further complicated the deterrence landscape. Threats of massive retaliation do not matter much for new nuclear nations aspiring to protect themselves from intimidation, but with rare intentions to strike first.[10] Nuclear weapons denote prestige and leverage to most aspirants, and for some, they entail a resistance to hegemony.

Second, the proliferation of missile systems and delivery capabilities threaten strategic balance as the threshold of reach and impact are being redefined by emerging military powers. Their ability to strike first and trigger brinkmanship with such capabilities challenges traditional deterrence stability notions. Third, there were greater instabilities being generated in nuclear-armed regions, especially in South Asia, where nuclear

---

9 Frank P. Harvey, "The Future of Strategic Stability and Nuclear Deterrence," *International Journal*, 58(2), Spring 2003.

10 While withdrawing from the ABM Treaty, President Bush asserted that "rogue" states are not deterred by assured destruction or massive retaliation. See Remarks at the National Defence University, Washington, 1 May 2001, available at http://www.fas.org/nuke/control/abmt/news/010501bush.html, accessed April 2012.

brinkmanship has been effectively used to promote conventional security interests. The scope for quick escalation to nuclear levels from conventional conflicts is rated as high in such regions, which demands countenance to offensive deterrence strategies.[11] Fourth, Cold War-type security competitions no longer exist as a polycentric world throws up a handful of major powers that would not risk a nuclear war, but could sufficiently invest in strategies and technologies to mitigate one.

These trends confirm a strategic transformation which favours a shift to qualitative deterrence rather than quantitative enhancements of offensive forces. A momentum in favour of nuclear reductions as incremental steps towards disarmament also complements this imperative. While major nuclear powers are taking steps to modernize nuclear weapons as sleek and mean machines, there is a general acceptance that an environment of defence dominance will contribute to global stability. Missile defences have emerged in this context as a preferable instrument that could help address the perceived deterrence gap among nuclear weapon states, or uneven advantages held through offensive forces. However, the dynamics of missile defence might throw up greater surprises on the deterrence impact beyond a qualitative shift.

---

11 Theoretical schools like proliferation/deterrence optimists and pessimists argue of a stability-instability paradox wherein competitive nuclear powers could embark on actions that could cause instability at the conventional and sub-conventional level while generally maintaining stability at the nuclear level. While the optimists argue that nuclear weapons have secured this equation by restricting conflict to the lowest tiers, pessimists feel the scope for escalation and brinkmanship could be high and rapid. For more on the debate, see Michael Krepon, "The Stability-Instability Paradox, Misperception and Escalation Control in South Asia," May 2003, at www.stimson.org/southasia/pdf/kreponmay03.pdf, accessed April 2013; Sumit Ganguly, "Indo-Pakistani Nuclear Issues and the Stability/Instability Paradox," *Studies in Conflict and Terrorism*, Vol.18, 1995; P.R. Chari, et.al, (eds.), *Nuclear Stability in Southern Asia*, New Delhi: Manohar, 2003; Varun Sahni, "The Stability-Instability Paradox," in E. Sridharan (ed.), *The India-Pakistan Nuclear Relationship*, New Delhi: Routledge, 2007.

The Dynamics of Missile Defence

There are various comparative scenarios that stimulate thinking in favour of a defensive strategy. When there is parity, the strategy will be not to trigger or provoke a war or attack with a balance or equity of strategic forces encouraging stability. When (defensive) weakness prevails, the strategy could be again not to provoke an attack, prepare to absorb an attack, and strengthen capability to retaliate, among others. When the offence is strong, the strategy will be to gain advantage and/or pre-empt the adversary's capabilities through a first strike. By that standard, it could be presumed that the nuclear-armed state having "perfect" defences holds the advantage, and can coerce the other even in a scenario of parity or existential deterrence. Even when there is parity of offence forces, the side without defences portrays a "window of vulnerability" to a first strike or the inability to pre-empt the first strike considering its own lack of defences and the other's ability to defend against retaliation.

On the other hand, the notions about missile defence as well as their utilities, character and implications, have not radically transformed despite the technological progress since their initiation in 1950/60s. The fundamental argument behind the rejection of ABM systems then was that a nuclear-armed state will gain defensive depth with its missile defence systems which will encourage it to strike first, either as a military expedition or to pre-empt the adversary. Conversely, by introducing an ABM system, a possessing state could have mounted the losses of an adversary whose attack could have lesser chances of success and also risks in-kind retaliation as a response. Interestingly, these fundamentals have not changed when ballistic missile defences, as a resurrected form of ABMs, have emerged in the post-Cold War strategic environment. Unlike the ABM phase, the current BMD era places emphasis on accuracy and precision, with better tracking systems and kill mediums even if their complete effectiveness in real conditions is still doubted.[12] The advantage

---

12 The evolution of these technologies is mentioned in Chapter I. For a detailed overview, see A. Vinod Kumar, "Ballistic Missile Defences in 2030: Trends

gained by the possession of missile defence systems for a nuclear-armed state is, however, tremendous, at least in terms of posturing and perception, and could tilt the equation in its favour. The perceptible scenarios of a BMD matrix in a nuclear environment could be illustrated thus:

> A nuclear-armed state, when in possession of a reasonably-effective BMD system, gains the advantage to attack first and also provide for defence against potential retaliation. Accordingly, the same state could also aspire to defend against a first strike/attack from the adversary, and protect its second-strike assets in order to retaliate.

> Such advantage gives natural incentives for a nuclear-armed state to attack its adversary which is not armed with defensive capabilities. The absence of this capability places a rival nuclear-armed state in a disadvantageous position and negates the deterrence depth of its offensive forces.

> A one-sided contest where only one state has BMD capability thus creates a force imbalance or strategic disequilibrium which could lead to instability. In a scenario where two rival nuclear states have missile defences, a natural strategic stalemate prevails, which provides scope for a new deterrence equation as well as opportunities to create strategic stability.

The complexities of a BMD-induced theatre are invariably influenced by the strategic environment and the nature of capability distribution. However, their dynamics would depend on two vital technological factors: (a) the ability of the missile defence systems to endow fool-proof interception, and (b) the wherewithal available with the adversary to counter the BMD system, either for an offensive charge that could overwhelm and/or put strain on the defences, or judicious engagement of countermeasures and decoys that could render a major part of the defences

in Technology Development," in Ajey Lele et.al (eds.), *Asia 2030* (New Delhi: Lancer International, 2010).

ineffective. Considering the fact the technology has not matured to a stage where comprehensive (either fool-proof or secure from countermeasures) interception capability can be assured, missile defences are still to provide the kind of defensive depth that could drastically alter the nature of the deterrence structure—although their influence on deterrence equations have remarkably risen along with major advances in interception technology and an increase in the number of nuclear-armed states acquiring them. The element that still remains in the realm of speculation is their qualitative impact on the addition to the strategic forces, and the overall outcomes for nuclear deterrence and strategic stability in a scenario where major nuclear powers compete to seek qualitative enhancement of their strategic forces through missile defences.

Is a new deterrence arrangement probable?

Mutually assured destruction was based on the understanding that countries will be deterred by their vulnerability to a retaliatory strike as a response to their first strike. The fundamental impact caused by the BMD capability of a possessing state could be to *increase the costs* of a first strike to the aggressor by raising prospects of its failure and, at the same time, promising massive retaliation in return. In other words, it is not just that the *cost* of undertaking the first strike will be increased by assured retaliation when second-strikes assets are protected, but also that its intended *gains* could be *diminished* when the first strike is countered. At the other end of the spectrum, the BMD-possessing state has incentives to escalate to a nuclear first strike in a conventional conflict with the confidence that a prospective retaliation from the adversary could have higher chances of being countered. Consequently, restraint will be a forced option for a state without BMD capability, while the consequences of such restraint will be disadvantageous in strategic and competitive terms considering that the BMD-armed rival could have intimidation propensity and escalation gains in conflict situations. When taken as a whole, the BMD-armed state will add these values to accumulate a greater deterrent capability which could be effectively projected along with its will to use them in an environment of its offensive dominance. Such balancing could be menacing, and cause instant security dilemma for the state without a BMD capability. This could amount to its deterrence failure which could force it to either counter the BMD through a massive offensive upsurge or by acquiring similar defensive capability, thus aggravating the competition.

Thus, it becomes evident that a compounding deterrence value could be generated in favour of the state armed with missile defences. Yet, the efficacy of the deterrence augmentation would realistically depend on the assessment of the other state of the rival's defensive depth, and its own self-confidence to counter it or its own acceptance of being deterred. This assessment eventually matters in concluding whether the rival's defensive force endows a deterrence value or not. Linked to this question is the quantum of technological variables that define the capability of the BMD systems in question, including their range, kill vehicles, interception record, numerical deployment, and projected coverage, among others. While advanced or longer-range endo-atmospheric systems (range within Earth's atmosphere) and mid-course exo-atmospheric systems (outside atmosphere) are known to endow comprehensive or nation-wide coverage, the enduring question of how much is enough to counter an offensive force is subject to actual conflict scenarios.

➢ In a conceivable scenario where BMD systems will be nominally deployed, without the record of optimal efficacy or total interception, the entry of even one missile into the territory without being intercepted could entail a success for the aggressor.

➢ For a scenario where BMD systems are employed with greater confidence of interception accuracy, the rival's deployment of countermeasures, the extensive use of multiple independently targeted re-entry vehicles (MIRVs) along with an ICBM "onslaught" can still challenge the BMD system from optimal performances.

Considering these possibilities, in the current technological evolutionary stage, it might be premature to establish the actual extent of the deterrence impact of BMD systems. Nonetheless, their ability to create a psychological advantage in an offence-defence balance cannot be denied. For, every nuclear power will find the defensive depth of rivals as a disadvantage for itself, thus prompting it to pursue a similar technology in spite of its relative confidence to overwhelm the systems of the rival. This acquisition push could create a domino effect, which could be the innate outcome of the security dilemma caused by the monopolistic advantage that BMD possessing states hold. Two case-examples can provide empirical evidence of such potential.

(a) BMD in US Deterrence Postures:

While the Americans have generally abstained from over-emphasising the deterrence potential of SDI systems in their nuclear posturing, the Bush administration sounded an exception by being specific about the need to reconfigure deterrence through missile defences. The decision to exit from ABM Treaty was intended to close vulnerabilities and integrate missile defences with offensive forces in order to augment deterrence, which seemed unviable when solely based on retaliation. Three specific deterrence roles were envisioned for BMD systems: first, they should deny adversaries any opportunity to attack the US; second, they should discourage/dissuade nations from acquiring missiles by diminishing their utility; third, they should deter the use of missiles by assuring that the costs of attack will outweigh intended gains. In other words, missile defences in US strategy are intended to achieve four objectives: *assure* allies, *dissuade* countries with missile projects, *deter* their use by denying benefits, and *defend* US interests comprehensively.[13] The strategy propounds the assessment that Cold War rivals have been supplanted by new proliferators as the emerging and potent threat factor. However,

---

13 Peppi DeBiaso, "Proliferation, Missile Defence and Conduct of Modern War," *Comparative Strategy*, Vol.25, 2006.

critics argue that the integration of "unreliable" BMD systems could only aggravate the security dilemma, and further encourage proliferation.[14]

Despite attempts to assure that US BMD will not affect Russian or Chinese deterrents, both countries resisted the deployment of US interceptors and radars in their backyard (Eastern Europe and East Asia) and had announced their intention to overwhelm US BMD through massive offensive thrusts. Along with its *Topol-M* ICBM, Russia has announced a new system that it claims could endow deep penetration of defences along with multiple offensive roles.[15] Despite its long-standing opposition to missile defence, China has gone on to challenge the equations by first testing a BMD system in January 2010 and following it up with another in 2013 and 2018.[16] Chinese offensive forces, on the other hand, historically drove India's nuclear plans besides driving India's own efforts to create a BMD capability against Chinese missiles with a range over the Indian hinterland.

(b) BMD in the South Asian Nuclear Dynamics:

India's response to Chinese postures is customarily seen as menacing to Pakistan, which strives for a capability equation. Pakistan has often expressed deep apprehension on the Indian BMD project, driven by the fact that such capability will weaken its deterrent and undermine the potency of its posturing. This nuclear relationship is imbalanced by the fact that unlike India's

---

14 Yousaf Butt, "The myth of missile defence as a deterrent," *Bulletin of the Atomic Scientists*, 8 May 2010.

15 Besides intending to overwhelm defences through the new ICBMs, Russia clarified that their deployment sites will be protected by its ABM systems, thus seeking to gain both offence and defence advantages; see Michael Listner, "Russian Federation touts new ICBM," *Examiner*, 6 May 2011, at http://www.examiner.com/space-policy-in-national/russian-federation-touts-new-icbm, accessed April 2012. (This was well before President Putin's March 2018 unveiling of the new missile inventory, mentioned in the Preface.)

16 A. Vinod Kumar, "The Dragon's Shield: Intricacies of China's BMD Capability," *IDSA Issue Brief*, February 2010.

no-first-use (NFU) doctrine, Pakistan is ambiguous on its nuclear thresholds, designed thus to accrue comprehensive deterrence against India at all levels—sub-conventional, conventional, and nuclear. Though the Indian BMD eventually seeks to attain the range and capability to counter Chinese medium-range missiles, its conceived ability to counter a Pakistani first-strike directly challenges the fundamental objective of the latter's deterrence. India could thus aspire to use its BMD to correct the imbalance created by Pakistan's postures by negating Pakistan's first-strike advantage as also ensuring the survivability of its own retaliatory forces. When Pakistan's nuclear deterrence centred on first use is eroded, India could also gain the advantage for a pre-emptive strike, emboldened by the assurance of undercutting Pakistan's retaliation. For a country with rudimentary air defence, Pakistan would be placed on a technological asymmetry by the Indian BMD. Some observers have argued that Pakistan too could acquire BMD systems to counter this. Though this could be to replicate the capability-balancing model pursued by Russia and China, the efficacy of this pursuit could be the relative propensity to undertake a first-strike—which though is limited considering India's NFU posture. Instead, by obstructing any advantage Pakistan sees from its first-strike posture, the Indian BMD seeks to skew the balance in its favour.

The two cases are evidence of how the introduction of missile defence can complicate deterrence arrangements, and be the cause for security dilemmas in nuclear relationships. The degree or nature of impact can, however, be debated. Various arguments could be made to establish the influence—negative or positive—on existing deterrent structures or the potential generation of new deterrence dynamics. There are could also be arguments to justify the negligible or limited impact on existing deterrence frameworks. That missile defence will shape the character of strategic stability is a foregone conclusion. In fact, at least for some states, missile defence might seem to be a rational defensive choice in an ambiguous state of deterrence as a tool of comprehensive defence.

For others, missile defence adds to the offensive aggregate and challenges the existing deterrence equations through asymmetric advantage to the beholder. Eventually, whether missile defences create a defensive balance or offence dominance will be the determinant to figure out its actual impact on nuclear deterrence and strategic relationships.

CHAPTER - IV

OFFENCE-DEFENCE BALANCE AND MISSILE DEFENCE

A useful framework to understand the impact of missile defence could be the offence-defence theory and its determinant, the offence-defence balance. The purpose of this chapter will not be to evaluate the merits of the theory but to understand whether its framework will help in determining the character of missile defence and its influence on deterrence and stability.

The fundamental premise of the theory, as generically accepted among its proponents, is that when the offence has dominance in inter-state relations, it could lead to competition and war; and when the balance favours defence, countries will be prompted to seek cooperation and peace. A tremendous body of literature has emerged on this concept, with origins traced to Clausewitz, best exemplified by his classical thinking on defence: "To preserve is easier than to acquire; the means on both sides being equal, the defensive is easier than the offensive." The superiority of defence leaves both sides with no incentive to attack. This was followed by many modern-day expositions on offence-defence interactions.[1]

---

1 Carl von Clausewitz, *On War*, translation by J.J. Graham, Hertfordshire: Wordsworth Editions Limited, 1997. Other modern day analyses include B.H.L. Hart's assessment that "any strengthening of the defensive at the expense of the offensive is a discouragement to aggression." Q. Wright's contention that superiority of offence will result in the probability of war and expansion while the superiority of defence decreases the decisiveness of war; and G.H. Quester pronouncing that offence produces war and defence

That missile defence blend with the Clausewitzian strategies is evident from his prognosis: "when one has used defensive means successfully, a more favourable balance of strength is usually created; thus the natural course in war is to begin defensively and end by attacking." Some interpretations of the Clausewitzian texts point out how defensive (retaliatory) deterrent strategies may be dependent on the same weapons that offensive (pre-emptive) strategies are, like in the case of missiles and missile defences or strategic missiles like ICBMs used for both purposes.[2] Defensive and offensive strategies, as per Clausewitzian thought, are defined by the political aim for which they are designed. The side which fears an attack (including pre-emption) and so shoots first may be said to be acting defensively, even if using missiles or weapons of mass destruction, and acting first. On the other hand, pre-emption may not appear rational unless the first striker expects to escape from destruction in retaliation.

It is, however, Robert Jervis who is credited with a systematic shaping of the offence-defence theory, especially using the concept of security dilemma—that an increase in one state's security decreases the security of others.[3] To understand this, he uses two approaches: distinguishing offensive weapons from defensive ones; and understanding whether the offence or the defence has the advantage (balance). While Jervis, as well as other theorists,

---

support peace. See B.H.L. Hart, "Aggression and Problem of Weapons," *English Review,* 55, 1932 (quoted by, Levy); Q. Wright, *A Study of War,* Revised Edition, Chicago: Chicago University Press, 1965, and G.H. Quester, *Offense and Defence in the International System,* New York: Wiley, 1977.

2   Stephen J. Cimbala, *Clausewitz and Escalation: Classical Perspective on Nuclear Strategy,* New York: Frank Cass, 1991.

3   Robert Jervis, "Cooperation under the Security Dilemma," *World Politics,* 30(2), January 1978. Other important analytical works that followed his formulations were Stephen Van Evera, "Offense, Defence and the Causes of War," *International Security,* 22(4), Spring 1998; Charles L. Glaser and Chaim Kaufmann, "What is the Offense-Defence Balance and Can we Measure it?", *International Security,* 22(4), Spring 1998; Sean M. Lynn-Jones, "Offense-Defence Theory and Its Critics," *Security Studies,* 4(4), Summer 1995; Keir A. Lieber, "Grasping the Technological Peace: The offense-Defence Balance and International Security," *International Security,* 25(1), Summer 2000, etc.

endorse the difficulty in establishing the differentiation as well as ascertaining the shift of the balance, it is quite fundamental to confirm the degree of the shift and the magnitude of the balance to understand the implications of a particular strategic matrix.[4]

The concept of offence-defence balance has been defined, described, and interpreted in various ways. Jervis states that when the offence has the advantage, "it is easier to destroy the other's army and take territory than it is to defend one's own," and when the defence has the advantage, "it is easier to protect and hold than to destroy and take (territory)." He contends that when defence has the advantage, "a large increase in a state's security only slightly decreases the security of others," and when the advantage of offence increases, the security dilemmas becomes more severe, arms races more intense, and war more likely. Jervis raises four conditions to describe the balance: (a) whether a state has to spend more or less on defence to offset a similar amount spent by the rival on offence, (b) to increase its security, should a state spend on offensive or defensive forces; (c) with its given inventory, whether it should attack or defend?; (d) is there an incentive to strike first or instead to absorb the other's blow? The argument highlights the relative advantage a state perceives from its resources to be able to defend or attack, based on what it feels as maximizing its security. Later day analyses have come out with clearer articulations on the balance. Glaser and Kaufmann, for example, define the balance as "the cost ratio of attacker forces to defender forces,"[5] while Lieber puts it more succinctly as the "relative ease" or the relative cost and benefits of attacking versus defending.[6] Lynn-Jones calibrates it in terms of "the number of resources that a state must invest in the offence to offset an adversary's investment in defence, or vice-versa.[7]

Jervis' uses two core variables—technology and geography— to identify the balance and the magnitude of its shift, while others

---

4   Jervis, Ibid.

5   Glaser and Kaufmann, n.3.

6   Lieber, n.3.

7   Lynn-Jones, n.3.

have expanded into broader variables, although this has been referred to as more of state-centric than as systemic factors. The chapter tries to apply BMD as the core technological variable to assess how it shifts the balance, and whether its introduction creates an offence or a defence advantage. The set of other features and propositions that are variedly used to explain the balance could be applied in a BMD environment as well. The crux of this chapter, however, is to understand three major implications of missile defence—*security dilemma, deterrence, role and character.*

Offence advantage creates security dilemma and arms race— Jervis states that when offence dominates, the incentives for pre-emption and the reciprocal fear of surprise attack increases. "There is no way for the state to increase its security without menacing or attacking the other." As stated in the previous section, a BMD-armed state, with the self-belief of defending its territory from retaliation, will have the incentives to attack first or pre-empt an impending attack by the adversary. This characteristic might be tempting to classify missile defences as creating an offence advantage. The argument made here is that: although missile defence might present itself as a purely defensive system, its combined use or projection with offence systems for an offensive purpose could enable it becoming instrumental in favouring an offence balance. Accordingly, when a state is encouraged by its monopolistic acquisition of a BMD system with the objective of pursuing an offensive strategy, it could cause its rivals to feel less secure and force them to enhance their own defensive capabilities, which could be by either building a similar defence capability or developing an offensive capability that could increase its defensive balance (capability to retaliate).

The possibility of offensive weapons contributing to a defensive balance is inherent in the framework if we consider that the state actually undertakes that investment for a defensive purpose. However, whether that state manages to achieve a defensive advantage would depend on the degree to which the rival state is deterred. Likewise, to create defence dominance with missile defences would be to envision a scenario wherein a BMD-armed state is able to withstand a first-strike by an adversary, protect its territory, and its retaliatory forces. It could be considered defence dominance if the state manages to ward off the rival with an offensive motive. As Jervis said, when the defence is dominant, wars are likely to be won only at an enormous cost as relatively weaker states can hold off or deter attack by raising the costs of conquest, which a missile defence system will be also able to provide for.[8] Hence, it could be assumed that in a BMD-dominant environment, there are possibilities for both offence and defence balancing, and it could invariably depend on the role envisaged by the country holding this capability—be it to empower/strengthen its offence forces or to counter an attack with a defensive role.

Will an offensive balance or defensive balance favour deterrence? As shown in the previous argument, a missile defence system may not just add to the net offensive capability of a state and contribute to an offensive dominance to the BMD-possessing state, but could also favour a defensive advantage by strengthening its defence. However, it needs to be ascertained in which of these equations a missile defence system would be causal for or contribute to deterrence. The deterrence discourse of the Cold War period points to its flexible and vibrant application in both defensive and offensive environments. In the 1970s, Jervis had a different take on the offence-defence roles of strategic forces. He argued that while the first strike on a counter-force target will be an offensive posture with a pre-emptive character, the second strike on a counter-value target by its inherent nature of being a retaliatory attack should be treated as defensive.[9] Thereby, in an equation of mutual vulnerability, retaliatory forces should be seen as defensive tools. Jervis buttresses this by identifying Inter-Continental Ballistic Missiles (ICBMs) as systems with innate offensive (first strike) and defensive roles (second strike), while Submarine-Launched Ballistic Missiles (SLBMs) as a survivable retaliatory force should be treated purely as defensive. By their inherent nature of being offensive and also used for retaliation, these systems are intrinsically supposed to be deterring their adversaries. Nuclear weapons, many believe, have

---

8   Jervis, n.3.

9   Ibid.

made deterrence the functional equivalent to defence.[10] Rather, the nuclear revolution has shifted the balance toward defence, as nuclear retaliatory forces make conquest prohibitively costly and hence weaker states armed with nuclear weapons could use it to deter stronger states, thus meeting both defence and deterrence—or rather, also defence through deterrence.[11]

However, there is a contrarian view that defence and deterrence are different, and that deterrence could be identified with punishment and hence has an offensive nature. Kenneth Waltz maintained that the ends of defence and deterrence are different, though dissuasion is a common means. Deterrence is achieved when there is a capability to punish, and a purely deterrence force will provide no defence.[12] Defences, he argued, are made to counter an intended attack through forces that look forbiddingly strong, and cannot be easily destroyed. By Waltz's argument, missile defence will inherently be a defensive capability which could dissuade an adversary from breaching the defences owing to the huge costs involved. But, Waltz did not account for how a country could use missile defences with the cumulative strength of its offensive forces to dissuade a country from attack. As shown earlier, a BMD+ICBM/SLBM force projection could invariably deter a country from initiating the first attack, and could also even discourage it from retaliation owing to a low confidence of breaching the defences. Hence, the deterrence value of missile defences in both offensive and defence dominance scenarios could be evenly accounted for.

So, are missile defences defensive or offensive? The equally vibrant roles missile defences play in offensive and defensive balancing could lead to nomenclature confusion—should it be termed as instruments of offensive defence or of defensive offence? An analogy could be drawn with ancient fortifications.

---

10 Lieber, n.3.

11 Lynn-Jones, n.3.

12 Waltz, "More may be better", in Scott D. Sagan and Kenneth N. Waltz, *The Spread of Nuclear Weapons: A Debate Renewed* (New York & London: W.W. Norton & Company, 2003).

Will a fortification that helps to repel an attack be an offensive or defensive balancer? How will the balance tilt when offensive forces are used to counter the same attack which the fortification helps to defend against in the first place? In both cases, it will be a defensive balance as the objective and role are defensive. But what if the fortification encourages the king to attack a neighbour with the confidence that his territory will not be breached? Or what if the combined strength of the offensive forces and a strong fortification is projected to the adversary in order to deter it? In both these cases, it is not just defence dominance but also a projection of an offensive posture using defences as the catalyst.

The same logic could apply to missile defences, with the key driving factors being the objective of the military mission, the role and character being assigned to the defensive force, and the intended outcome of the mission. A causal (or even outcome) of this definitional complexity is the inability to differentiate missile defences as an offence or defence balancer. Jervis and others have pondered on this difficulty, which was also illustrated by the ICBM and SLBM differentiation. Interestingly, Jervis had, in this assessment, termed active and passive defences, including city defences that protect against counter-value targeting, as predominantly offensive, while likening the hardening of missile silos and warning systems as defensive postures.[13] Lynn-Jones suggests the insignificance of such differentiation as the balancing happens as a continuum depending on strategic considerations. "States formulate their security strategies on the basis of their perceptions of the offence-defence balance,"[14] which also implies that a defensive weapon could also be *perceived* as providing an offensive balance in particular circumstances. Distinguishing between offensive and defensive weapons has been a policy nightmare since the 1932–33 Geneva Disarmament Conference where countries could not agree on which weapon is offensive or defensive.[15] It has, therefore, been of general acceptance that roles

---

13 Jervis, n. 3.

14 Lynn-Jones cites the ICBM silo as a perfect example of a defensive technology (hardened silo) protecting an offensive weapon (nuclear warheads). See, n.3.

15 Levy quotes the Naval Commission of the League of Nations Conference

assigned to a weapon combined with the military and political objective will determine the character of a weapon system. The same predicament might figure in terming missile defence as providing for an offensive utility or as a purely defensive system, or with conceptual incarnations of offensive defence or defensive offence. This volume largely favours terming the impact from the large-scale deployment of missile defences as creating an offensive defence.

Argument: *Missile defences are instruments of security maximization that could accentuate offence dominance by adding to the net offensive capability of strategic forces.*

In spite of an overarching nuclear non-proliferation regime and a cornerstone instrument (Treaty on the Non-Proliferation of Nuclear Weapons or NPT) prevailing over the affairs of nuclear trade and the proliferation of technologies, (very) few normative instruments actually exist to control or streamline the usage of nuclear weapons or missile systems with actual usage left to the politics of nuclear-armed states and their strategic actions. Considering that missile defence could operate or will be introduced into this milieu, a handful of catalytic reasons could be listed to explain its potential impact, include how it could favour an offensive balance, contribute to deterrence, and be causal for security dilemma and the arms race.

1. *Self-help system* – In a supposedly anarchic world driven by national interests, missile defences emerge as a self-help system for states confronted with vulnerabilities and left to fend for themselves. In order to address their security challenges, states that perceive inherent weaknesses will be encouraged to depend on such systems through their unilateral acquisition as a means to counter/negate the offensive advantage held by their rivals. Further,

for the Reduction and Limitation of Armament statement on the dilemma: supposing a state undertakes armed aggression through offensive operation, what are the weapons, which, by their specific character, are likely to enable a rapid conclusion to the aggression? Jack S. Levy, "The Offensive/Defensive Balance of Military Technology: A Theoretical and Historical Analysis," *International Studies Quarterly*, Vol. 28, 1984.

offensive forces being intrinsically potent and drivers of security dilemmas and with the absence of treaties to safeguard against the potential breach of vulnerabilities, the acquisition of a defensive capability could be deemed as an imperative pursuit of security.

2. *Security maximization and comprehensive defence* – Though missile defences could be preferred to spearhead a defensive strategy or to be postured with offensive forces complementing the retaliatory role, countries with a missile defence system and operating in a volatile environment could use such capability as a means to maximize their security, and provide comprehensive homeland protection to their territories. When proactive objectives like lessening opportunities of enemy attack, conquest, or maximizing technological resources determine security policy and postures, it is more likely that missile defences will be introduced to provide offensive forces with a support system that could allow them to provide a defensive depth, thus justifying their identity as an offensive defence.

3. *Deterrence* – As argued earlier, security maximization will not just restrict to a defensive role or complementing offensive forces with defensive depth, but also exploring means to ensure that the defensive capability is sufficiently projected and deployed to deter potential adversaries. For this to happen, missile defences might be postured alongside offensive forces as a net offensive capability in order to project a cumulative and comprehensive deterrent force.

4. *Net offensive capability* – Despite being defensive systems, the inherent potential of missile defences to contribute to the net offensive capability has been proven by new deterrence approaches of countries like the USA, which seeks to add a defensive layer to offensive deterrence. There are other factors as well that support the aggregation of missile defence with offensive strategies.

The incentive to strike first at an adversary (with or without defensive intentions), backed by defensive depth, provides the BMD-possessing state with the flexibility of strike options, deterrence utility, power profile enhancement, and strategic superiority, all of which could contribute to offence dominance.

5. *Technological opportunism* – Countries that develop or acquire a new technology may not be customarily inclined to use it for a defensive balance, and instead could use it to gain political and military advantage. This could be seen in the case of USA, which has optimally tried to use its missile defence postures to intimidate its rivals, attempt to change the strategic *status quo* (the GMDS deployment plan in Eastern Europe) in areas where it is in great power competition, or explore politico-diplomatic purposes (like pushing for East Asian theatre defences to put pressure on China and North Korea).

Missile Defence, Competition, and Arms Race

The dynamics of introducing missile defence into a strategic environment have been illustrated in the previous sections. The cursory assessment of the impact of missile defences on strategic stability was based on the offence-defence framework, which essentially postulates that when the offence is dominant, it could permeate a security dilemma causing nations to compete. Further, it has been demonstrated that missile defence could contribute to both offensive and defensive balancing. Unlike offensive forces, however, missile defences even when favouring a defensive balance can continue to cause or aggravate the security dilemma and competition. This could happen when the confidence of a state (without BMD capability) to impart a decisive first blow is diminished and instead fears retaliation which could menace this actor to pursue a similar capability or a countenance strategy to restore an offensive/defensive balance in its favour.

The new problem of stability emerges when the other state in a strategic equation also develops missile defences. It is the potential for a defensive symmetry and its implications that would explain the character of the competition and arms race in a strategic environment that could be shaped by increasing acquisition of this technology. The competition created by a missile defence imbalance, however, need not necessarily confine to a race for defensive capabilities, but could also affect the offensive equations as the enduring security dilemma will sustain an environment of suspicion about actual capabilities and intentions. The US-Soviet race for interception technologies during the Cold War was a testament to how a state can compete to develop both offensive and defensive capabilities when it fears that a combination of both adds to the offensive edge of the rival.

Nonetheless, it could be assumed that the arms races from an offence asymmetry could be aimed at achieving a counter-offensive advantage while the result of competition from a defensive imbalance might be to achieve a defensive symmetry. Two factors will influence such outcomes. First, the interregnum before the rival state acquires a BMD system would be one where the state with the first advantage will flexibly tilt the offence or defence balance as per convenience, thus creating a sustained environment of a security dilemma. Second, the nature of offence-defence balancing will be influenced by a degree of uncertainty on how each actor assesses the capabilities derived by the rival from both systems. In both cases, contest and competition will prevail as a continuum for an uncertain future until both actors are convinced of a defensive *status quo* and stable deterrence prevailing in the dyad or theatre. The potential and opportunities for deterrence stability in an equation of offensive and defensive symmetry should hence be explored, especially when defensive systems like missile defences vitiate an existing deterrence equation dominated by offensive forces.

Argument: *A (mutual) defensive deterrence arrangement can emerge between BMD-armed nuclear weapon states as a means to deterrence stability and to encourage arms control.*

The conceptual question, with policy implications, that needs to be addressed here is: Can the competition generated by the introduction of missile defences be politically managed through an effective arms control or deterrence balancing process? In fact, a key policy formulation offered by offence-defence theory is that "arms races and conflicts may be prevented through carefully designed arms control agreements that either deliberately shifts the balance of technology towards defence or seek to correct misperceptions of the balance."[16] Offence-defence theorists largely place this potential on the ability of states to calibrate their forces towards a defence balance and conveying to adversary their lack of offensive intent or clearing misperceptions on postures.[17] A poser at this stage could be whether missile defences have technologically matured or politically emerged to a stage where their influence on offensive or defensive balancing can be managed and whether an arms control agreement or a loose arrangement could be explored. Also, an ABM-Treaty like measure to keep vulnerabilities open might no longer be feasible in the current strategic environment.

Nonetheless, there are multiple strategies that could be explored to manage a potential arms race caused by missile defences, including the charting of a new BMD-driven deterrence equation. The first such option will be when nuclear powers begin to agree that there can be near-parity of offensive and defensive forces that will tilt the balance neither in favour of offence dominance or defence advantage. The foremost objective of such balancing could be to endorse the formal jettisoning of mutual vulnerability as a strategic requirement of deterrence. The premise of such balancing will be the potential creation of missile defence symmetries alongside offensive forces. This could, however, require a uniform acquisition pattern or the possession of advanced interception capabilities by all the nuclear-armed states, or those in a competitive dyad, which looks probable if the current race is any indication. While the race for defensive platforms has not attained

---

16 Lieber, n.3.

17 While Jervis argues that offence and defence systems should be differentiated, which will help create arms control agreements to ban forces that cause an offence balance and security dilemmas, Van Evera calls for governments to adopt defensive force postures, and seeks arms control agreements to limit offensive forces.

the feverish element seen in the offensive realm, that some states (especially those who proliferated technologies to build nuclear forces) will struggle to make this breakthrough is proof that symmetries may not form as a natural evolution. On the other hand, there is the question of extended deterrence wherein dominant nuclear powers have to ensure defensive coverage to allies as intended by the US Phased Adaptive Approach[18] for Europe, and NATO's own missile defence platforms. New permutations— like China offering BMD coverage or technologies to Pakistan, and Russia doing a similar act for Iran—could make this aspect more competitive and prone to newer contests. Nonetheless, the creation of a defensive symmetry in a nuclear dyad is fundamental to the facilitation of a fresh deterrence equation whereby missile defences on both sides could limit the scope of first-use, and also restrict the potential for massive retaliation, which in itself could be a sustainable stabilising construct. When executed in a bilateral framework between two nuclear weapon states, this could intrinsically imply, and facilitate a (mutual) defensive deterrence equation.

The second option will be a revisiting of the attempts by the Geneva Disarmament Conference of 1932–33 to differentiate offensive weapons from the defensive ones. Though it might look premature and unrealistic at this stage of technological evolution and an uncertain strategic milieu, this would be one fruitful approach to complement the nuclear disarmament efforts or the phased reduction processes pursued by at least some nuclear powers. An understanding that missile defences have to be normatively and operationally classified as defensive systems and to be used purely for defensive purposes could entail their postural separation from the offensive forces, which are, in turn, considered for phased reductions. A major spin-off of such classification could be envisioned in a nuclear reduction scenario where missile

---

18 Shifting from the original deployment plan in Poland and Czech Republic, the new approach intends a segregated mobile deployment across Europe. See, *Fact Sheet on U.S. Missile Defence Policy*, The White House, 17 September 2009, at http://www.whitehouse.gov/the_press_office/FACT-SHEET-US-Missile-Defence-Policy-A-Phased-Adaptive-Approach-for-Missile-Defence-in-Europe/, accessed September 2015.

defences can act as a stabilizer or guarantor of security when countries are encouraged to pursue offensive armament reduction in an atmosphere of trust and credible verifications. In the long run, we could envision a scenario when the balancing of missile defence capabilities might devalue the gains of deterrence, and encourage the durable reduction of offensive forces, potentially leading to their total elimination. One could relevantly recall President Reagan's SDI speech in this context.

"I am directing a comprehensive and intensive effort to define a long-term research and development program to achieve our ultimate goal of eliminating the threat posed by strategic nuclear missiles. This could pave the way for arms control measures to eliminate the weapons themselves... Our only purpose—one all people share—is to search for ways to reduce the danger of nuclear war."[19]

---

19 Text of President Reagan's SDI speech of 23 March 1983, available at: http://www.atomicarchive.com/Docs/Missile/Starwars.shtml, accessed September 2015.

Chapter - V

Missile Defence in the Southern Asian Theatre

<hr/>

The composite region termed as Southern Asia has been a dynamic theatre of nuclear interplay with the unique presence of three nuclear-armed states—China, India and Pakistan.[1] Ever since the first Chinese nuclear test in 1964, nuclear weapons have invariably shaped the strategic contours of this region, which was further conditioned by the nuclear weapon pursuits of Pakistan and India. While China strove to calibrate its deterrent against its perceived rivals (initially the Americans, and later also the Soviets) during the four decades of its nuclear monopoly in the Southern Asian region, the India-Pakistan deterrence equation began to effectively take shape after both nations embarked on a series of nuclear tests in May 1998, and declared their intention to achieve credible minimum deterrence. The subsequent years were marked by an intense build-up of nuclear arsenals, with China pursuing a strategic modernisation effort even as India and Pakistan raced to fulfil the primary pre-requisites of what they perceived as "credible" and "minimum" deterrence.

<hr/>

1 Southern Asia is not a geographical description that is often seen in Western nuclear-related literature, which has pre-occupied itself on the China-US strategic competition as well as the India-Pakistan (South Asian) nuclear relationship. Considering that the China-India and the India-Pakistan nuclear dyads cannot be treated in isolation, this volume seeks to describe the composite region as Southern Asia.

Meanwhile, the advent of the various components of the US missile defence system since the late 1990s also began to influence the strategic calculus of the region. Though India was supposedly the first among the three to begin work on missile defence technologies, China was also by then synchronising its responses to American missile defence initiatives that were beginning to impact the security environment in its neighbourhood. For over a decade after Washington's announcement of its layered BMD plan,[2] Beijing publicly and vociferously opposed the very idea of missile defences, terming them as a cause for an arms race and the militarization of space. Remarkably though, China thereafter set forth on its own missile defence and anti-satellite (ASAT) programmes as part of its active defence strategy. On the other hand, India is believed to have launched its missile defence programme in the late 1990s (as a response to China-Pakistan missile cooperation) probably around the same time it was galloping towards overt nuclearisation. As the third player in this matrix, Pakistan spent its energies on developing an India-centric nuclear deterrent, along with the acquisition of high-end conventional capabilities, which it believed could deter India comprehensively. However, in the process, Pakistan seems to have spared few resources to devise a technological option as a response to the missile defence influx in its strategic periphery.

By most accounts, nuclear deterrence in Southern Asia (especially in the South Asian dyad) seems to have evolved to levels certainly beyond the rudimentary; but it is yet to reach a condition of adequacy that could be deemed as survivable and credible. Thus, should the introduction of missile defence in Southern Asia be seen as premature in this evolutionary curve? And if so, will it not complicate the evolving deterrence dynamics in this region rather than contribute to its consolidation or lead to deterrence

---

2 President George W. Bush sanctioned the US programme for a layered BMD programme which included the development and deployment of interception platforms that could shoot down enemy missiles in the boost, mid-course, and terminal phases. For a cursory description of US BMD programme, see http://www.mda.mil/system/system.html, accessed August 2013. Also see, "US Missile Defence Programs at a Glance," June 2013, at http://www. armscontrol.org/factsheets/usmissiledefence, accessed August 2013.

stability? Instead, should it be construed that the nuclear states pursuing missile defence expect to enhance deterrence by adding greater defensive depth through these platforms? The current picture remains unclear as the nuclear powers in the region are yet to grapple with the full dimensions of this technology. Indeed, they are still confronted with the dynamic transformations in the security environment which challenge the consolidation of their nuclear deterrence process.

Some inferences can be highlighted about this condition. First, despite different levels of capabilities and characteristically divergent approaches to deterrence, all three states are talking about their prevalent posture of minimum deterrence and consequently seeking to match the capabilities of their nuclear rivals. However, none have seemingly reached a position where they can confidently declare the acquisition of assured destruction or massive retaliation capability, which remains at the core of their nuclear doctrines (the no-first-use postures of China and India, or Pakistan's presumed intention to use nuclear weapons first). Second, even when theoretically convinced that their offensive (or survivable retaliatory) capabilities will determine the potency of their deterrent, the two states pursuing missile defence seems unclear in their public articulations about its operational space and doctrinal character in their strategic force planning. For that matter, it might seem early for them to define whether missile defence systems will provide them with an advantage of defensive depth (to protect against either a first strike or a retaliatory attack), or augment their deterrence postures against adversaries. In other words, even while working towards employing missile defences alongside their strategic forces, neither China nor India is articulate about whether they will be aiming at denial deterrence, or will use these defences to buttress retaliatory deterrence. As such, it would be easier to infer that the Southern Asian nuclear powers are confronted by a situation wherein the technology they have developed has preceded their strategic objectives and doctrinal requirements. This, however, may not be assumed to be a finite or uniform pattern if the Chinese and Indian strategic debates are assessed. While the world waits to understand the objectives of

China's missile defence programme after years of its opposition to this technology, the Indian security establishment is attempting to provide a definite meaning to this technological pursuit in its deterrence posture.

Deterrence in Southern Asia: The Space for Missile Defence

As states that were opposed to, or not initially poised towards missile defence, the current development progress attained by China and India opens questions about their evolving conceptions towards this technological platform, their intended objectives, and how their employment is likely to alter the strategic environment in the respective theatres. To start with, deterrence in Southern Asia is itself passing through a crucial evolutionary phase, embodied in the constant expansion of capabilities, doctrinal realignments, and divergent patterns of technological development and postural behaviour. Some postulations could be made to describe this.

> Despite varying capabilities and inventories, all three nuclear states seek to pursue the common objective of attaining credible minimum deterrence even if the definition of credibility, and what amounts to be minimum may not be uniform.

> Though each of the nuclear arsenals are galloping at an uninhibited pace, the assessments of individual nations of "what" and "how much" is needed to achieve credible minimum deterrence is not sufficiently articulated, and hence creates doubts, apprehensions, or misrepresentations about the credibility of these deterrents (the ambiguity could also be deliberate, to confuse the adversaries).

> While Pakistan as the sole state with a declared preference for first-strike options is unsure about its realistic thresholds, both India and China are increasingly confronted with various push and pull factors on the need to revisit or readjust their No-First-Use (NFU) doctrines in order to address their dynamic strategic environments, as also to increase confidence in the doctrines.

Two relevant questions that will be considered in the subsequent analysis are: do India and China foresee the possibility of missile defences giving them greater defensive depth and/or adding to their deterrence capabilities? Will Pakistan be forced to change its deterrence postures with the introduction of missile defence in the region? A country-wise assessment of deterrence postures and drivers of missile defence could give a clearer picture.

China: Between Minimum and Limited Deterrence?

At the outset, it is worth mentioning the nuclear setting in which China practices its nuclear deterrence. China has probably the most challenging nuclear environment in which it has to consider the presence and influence of at least five nuclear-armed states— Russia, the USA, India, North Korea, and Pakistan—while undertaking its strategic planning. China has friendly relations with only two of these nuclear-armed neighbours, followed by a history of hostility with two others (India and Russia), and considers the nuclear competition with the USA (and American extended deterrence coverage in its neighbourhood) as the primary threat condition. China's sustained force augmentation (strategic forces modernisation) and strategic support to North Korea and Pakistan create constant pressure on its competitive nuclear neighbours, with varied implications for each for them. This is the backdrop in which US missile defences have been introduced into China's periphery: first through theatre missile defence (TMD) systems deployed with its East Asian allies; and second, the ineluctable pressure created on China's nuclear deterrence with its longer-range missiles being susceptible to the US BMD mainstays, be it the GMDS in the American west coast or the EPAA systems covering the Eurasian frontlines. The Chinese riposte, with its own missile defence developmental posturing, though coming belatedly, has, however, complicated the nuclear deterrence calculus in the Asian region, which has two other actors (Russia and India) already surging forward in this new race.

Most of the available literature (not necessarily contemporaneous) on China's nuclear deterrence is dominated by Western notions about Chinese postures and capabilities, with some of them dealing with questions like why China had based its deterrent on a small and vulnerable retaliatory force for a long period and without an operational doctrine.[3] Highlighted in some texts is the prolonged reliance on a rather unsophisticated missile inventory, consisting of medium-range and interim-range missiles like the *Dong Feng* (DF)-2, -3 and -4, all liquid-fuelled, semi-mobile, and with low-penetration capability. The major shift in the attainment of strike capabilities was through DF-5 in the early 1980s, with over 12,000 km range to target the USA but with liquid-propellants and long preparation time. Despite improving on mobility and shifting to the solid propellant, even later systems like DF-21 and -31 were seen as no less vulnerable, with their huge support systems and dependence on pre-surveyed sites.

Besides factors like political chaos and tardy industrial culture being cited as the reasons for the slow progress in the early years, most observers attribute it to the attitude of first-generation leaders like Mao Zedong and Deng Xiaoping, who had termed nuclear weapons as "paper tigers" and symbolic.[4] Although they later embraced the utility of nuclear weapons as a means to deter "nuclear aggression and coercion" and not for warfighting, they came around to the belief that a posture of (assured) retaliation using a small number of survivable weapons could create deterrence against nuclear-armed adversaries. In fact, this perception of existential deterrence guided China's nuclear strategy for a long period, with a focus on creating a "certain power to strike back," not by numerical matching or precision but through weapons which are survivable, and had lesser preparation

---

3   Some of these analyses include M. Taylor Fravel and Evan S. Medeiros, "China's Search for Assured Retaliation," *International Security*, Vol. 35(2), Fall 2010; John Wilson Lewis and Hua Di, "China's Ballistic Missile Programs: Technologies, Strategies, Goals," *International Security*, Vol. 17, Autumn 1992; Keir A. Lieber and Daryl G. Press, "The Rise of U.S. Nuclear Primacy," *Foreign Affairs*, No. 85, March/April 2006, among others.

4   See the handful of original Chinese sources quoted by Wu Riqiang, "Certainty of Uncertainty: Nuclear Strategy with Chinese Characteristics," *Journal of Strategic Studies*, Vol. 36 (4), May 2013. Also see, Yao Yunzhu, "Chinese Nuclear Policy and the Future of Minimum Deterrence," in Christopher P. Twomey (ed.), *Perspectives on Sino-American Strategic Nuclear Issues*, New York: Palgrave Macmillan, 2008.

time in the event of a surprise nuclear attack.[5] However, this condition was to be transformed with the initiation of strategic modernisation traced to the 1990s, fuelled by remarkable economic growth and the impulses created by the post-Cold War environment. The process of strategic modernisation, though an ongoing process since its initiation, was initially aimed at: (a) augmenting the nuclear deterrent from "minimum" to "limited", and beyond; (b) developing a new generation of survivable second-strike capabilities that enables assured destruction and first-strike uncertainty; and (c) the possibility of doctrinal and postural changes to refine deterrence, and also to deal with conventional or non-nuclear attacks from adversaries.

Minimum or limited: Most analyses on the modernisation process debate whether China has achieved the ability to project "minimum" deterrence, or whether it targets a capability of "limited" deterrence.[6] The concept of minimum deterrence is defined as "threatening the lowest level of damage necessary to prevent an attack with fewest numbers of nuclear weapons."[7] Though the Chinese feel a small arsenal can provide minimum deterrence with the threat of unacceptable damage, it implies a qualitative threshold of "sufficiency" based on survivable retaliatory forces.[8] By most accounts, China is assumed to be rapidly moving towards this threshold, but not sufficient enough to be credible in the context of a variety of threats and the wide force matrix of adversaries, and also with shortcomings in

---

5   These principles were articulated by Gen. Zhang Aiping, who was defence minister in the 1980s. Original Chinese source quoted by Fravel and Medeiros, n.3.

6   See Fravel and Medeiros, n.3; also see, John Lewis and Xue Litai, "Evolution of China's Military Strategy Guidance and Nuclear Strategy, *Lingdaozhe*, No. 38 February 2011 (this article in Chinese language is quoted by Wu Riqiang, n. 4). Also see, Jing-dong Yuan, "Effective, Reliable and Credible: China's Nuclear Modernisation," *The Non-Proliferation Review*, Vol. 14 (2), 2007.

7   "Committee on the US-Chinese Glossary of Nuclear Security Terms," *English-Chinese, Chinese English Nuclear Security Glossary*, Washington, DC: National Academies Press, 2008.

8   Jing-dong Yuan, n.6.

survivability, precision, numbers, and mobility (which the current modernisation process seemingly aims to address).

However, another section of observers argues that China has had satisfactory levels of minimum deterrence and, since the 1990s, has been seeking to move towards limited deterrence.[9] Limited deterrence entails the acquisition of "limited warfighting capability to inflict costly damage on the adversary at every rung on the escalation ladder, thus denying the adversary victory in a nuclear war."[10] By most Chinese formulations, it is not any closer to such a capability and rather has a "self-defensive" posture, implying the absence of a nuclear warfighting plan. Alastair Johnston's formulation of limited deterrence includes capabilities like the more accurate Inter-Continental Ballistic Missiles (ICBMs); the Submarine-Launched Ballistic Missiles (SLBMs) as a counter-value force; theatre nuclear weapons; space-based assets; and missile defence; among others.[11] That many of these systems are integral elements in the ongoing modernization process indicates the desire to acquire a limited deterrence capability. However, China justifies such enhancements as a means to increase the credibility of its deterrent rather than about shifting to a new posture, howsoever it is described. Since 2006, China's white papers uniformly articulate the mission of "a self-defensive strategy (sic) to deter others from using or threatening to use nuclear weapons against China."

Assured destruction and first-strike uncertainty: Thus, the focus of strategic modernisation is seemingly geared towards making the arsenal more survivable against a first-strike through

---

9   The most notable work on China's limited deterrence thinking was by Alastair Iain Johnston in "China's New "Old Thinking": The Concept of Limited Deterrence," *International Security*, Vol. 20 (3), Winter 1995–1996. Jing-dong Yuan, Fravel and Medeiros, and Thomas J. Christensen have also examined in great depth the Chinese pursuit of limited deterrence. See, Thomas J. Christensen, "The Meaning of The Nuclear Evolution: China's Strategic Modernization and the US-China Security Relations," *Journal of Strategic Studies*, Vol.35 (4), 2012.

10   See n. 7.

11   See Johnston, n. 9.

numerical augmentation, greater mobility, and features like launch on warning (LoW) centred on tactically-mobile, more accurate, and faster solid-fuelled systems. These include upgraded solid-fuelled systems, like DF-21A and -31A, and SLBMs like *Julang* (JL)-2, besides submarine platforms of the *Jin* and *Xia*-class, as well as capabilities in manoeuvrable re-entry vehicles (MaRV), and multiple independently targetable re-entry vehicles (MIRV).[12] The new systems, the Chinese believe, will develop the capability for assured retaliation that will be on par with major nuclear powers, if not the USA. The Chinese also feel that a greater number of silo-based missiles, more and quieter SSBNs, and features like launch-on-warning combined with highly-mobile launchers could impart first-strike uncertainty for its adversaries.[13] Further, greater mobility and concealment measures could ensure that the adversary will not know the exact numbers and location of retaliatory forces, and thereby reduce their confidence in guaranteeing destruction from a pre-emptive strike.[14] Chinese planners believe that these capabilities will enable China to absorb a first-strike, and endow unacceptable damage on enemy assets.[15]

The NFU and postural realignments: Speculations have been rife in recent years regarding the possibility of China revising its No-First-Use (NFU) posture, or adding new conditions to this doctrine in order to enhance its deterrence depth. These debates are driven by two trends: (a) expressive changes in successive white papers, with new and novel articulations; and (b) a plethora of articles from the PLA staple with intense debates on the NFU provision. For example, the 2008 White Paper, while maintaining the usual slogans of self-defence and NFU, also talked about a "lean and effective deterrent and *flexible use of different means*

---

12 For more on the current status of the modernization process, see "Annual Report to Congress: Military and Security Developments involving the People's Republic of China 2013," Office of the Secretary of Defence, May 2012, at http://www.defence.gov/pubs/2013_china_report_final.pdf, accessed August 2013.

13 See Wu Riqiang, n. 4.

14 Ibid.

15 Fravel and Medeiros, n.3.

with expanded roles of the Second Artillery."[16] It also talks of going *into a state of alert*, and getting *ready* for a nuclear counterattack to *deter* the enemy from using nuclear weapons—a vague formulation (repeated in 2010 and 2012), considering how a "state of alert" and "getting ready" is realistically supposed to deter an enemy unless the intention, capability, and preparedness to "counterattack" is amply postured. While the new description in the 2008 White Paper could be natural posturing driven by new capabilities, the turning point was the 2012 White Paper which had no reference to NFU; instead, it stated that "we will not attack unless attacked and will counterattack if attacked." This, in fact, is akin to NFU, though not without raising alarm about why the description text was changed.

This was, however, seen as an outcome of the internal debates in China about the means to enhance deterrence, and making the NFU flexible for new strategic conditions.[17] This is because a scenario that China supposedly fears is that of the USA launching a conventional attack or using non-nuclear means like Prompt Global Strike and ballistic missile defences to neutralise China's retaliatory assets. With the NFU constraining a nuclear response to conventional strikes, prominent sections in the PLA supposedly believe that even its conventional response might be countered by American missile defences. This debate over the NFU was first reportedly initiated in 2005 by Major General Zhu Chenghu, demanding that China should use nuclear weapons if attacked with conventional forces.[18] Though such suggestions were then rejected, many voices in the PLA came around to the view that NFU constrains the flexibility of Chinese responses.

---

16 See, *China's National Defence in 2008*, released in January 2009, at http:// english.gov.cn/official/2009-01/20/content_1210227.htm, accessed August 2013.

17 'The PLA trilogy: The Science of Strategy' *Zhanlüexue*, May 1999; 'The Science of Campaigns', *Zhanyixue*, May 2000, and 'A Course of Study in Combined Arms Tactics', *Hetongzhanshuxuejiaocheng*; August 2000, are often quoted, alongside 'The Science of Second Artillery Campaigns', *Die rPaobing Zhanyixue*, 2004, to highlight such debates within the PLA.

18 Joseph Kahn, "Chinese General Threatens Use of A-Bombs if US Intrudes," *New York Times*, 15 July 2005.

There are various interpretations on the references in the *Dier Paobing Zhanyixue* about *lowering the nuclear threshold* and *anti-nuclear deterrence* which, some feel, indicates thinking in favour of a first-strike, even if Chinese scholars publicly reject such assumptions.[19] Such references, when correlated with vague statements in the white papers, underlined an intrinsic process of review and pressure for reforms in the doctrinal spectrum. The prevailing concern is whether the NFU "will survive any attempt to disable China's retaliatory capabilities," which, in other words, indicates the threat envelope that weighs down on China's NFU doctrinal structures.[20] A notable Chinese elucidation came from a military official in a journal article wherein it was stated that "China's NFU indicates its goal of minimum deterrence by threat of punishment, its self-defensive nature, application at the grand strategic level and not tactical levels, and dependence on uncertainty, etc."[21] The point conveyed here seems to be that China's nuclear weapons will be used only in a strategic context and for retaliation; though the references to "dependence on uncertainty" and "self-defence" could be variedly interpreted, especially in the light of the NFU review debate. Such perspectives notwithstanding, the general character of Chinese nuclear strategy seems to indicate the pursuit of multi-layered deterrence— entailing minimum deterrence against the USA and Russia, limited deterrence with regard to theatre nuclear forces, and a pre-emptive and counterforce posture through its conventional missile forces.[22]

China and Missile Defence

Two questions are relevant to this context: (a) China's approach towards US missile defence and (b) why China decided to develop

---

19 See Christensen, n. 9, and the response by Wu Riqiang, n. 4.

20 Fravel and Medeiros, n.3.

21 Sr. Col. Yao Yunzhu, "China's Perspectives on Nuclear Deterrence," *Air and Space Power Journal*, Spring 2010.

22 Bates Gill, James Mulvenon, and Mark Stokes, "The Chinese Second Artillery Corps: Transition to Credible Deterrence," in Richard Yang and James Mulvenon (eds.), *The People's Liberation Army as Organization: Reference Volume v1.0*, Santa Monica, CA: RAND, 2002.

missile defence systems. China becomes the classical case of how a state's perceptions are developed about missile defences— whether they are tilting the offence-defence balance, or providing an offensive advantage to the possessor, or affecting deterrence stability in a nuclear dyad when a rival acquires the capability. For, China perceives a direct challenge to its deterrent from the US layered missile defence architecture which, it feels, adds to the net deterrence capability of American strategic forces, and thus drives an instant security dilemma for itself. Hence, the initial Chinese reaction was to reject the notion of missile defences as a defensive system. As early as 2000, Ambassador Sha Zukang said that:

> ...the history of missile defence programmes and the acknowledged design capabilities of (NMD) show that the proposed system can be directed against China and can seriously affect China's limited nuclear capability.[23]

Thus, the threat matrix that China perceives can be described on the following lines:

➢ The US could launch a major pre-emptive conventional strike against Chinese retaliatory assets. A conventional Chinese response could be countered with considerable effectiveness by theatre defences in East Asia as well as sea-based interceptors from a proximate zone (PAC/THAAD and Aegis SM-3/6).

➢ Even if China was to respond with nuclear weapons to a conventional or a nuclear first-strike, the Chinese long-range missiles could be vulnerable to the interception reach of US mid-course systems (GMDS) deployed on the American west coast, whereas the nuclear-armed interim-range Chinese delivery systems could be targeted by the advanced endo-atmospheric interceptor platforms (THAAD and Aegis SM-3/6).

➢ US lower-tier air/theatre defence systems (PAC) in East Asia could counter Chinese short-range missiles if it decides to confront Taiwan, or other East Asian rivals.

---

23 Sha Zukang, "US Missile Defence Plans: China's View," *Disarmament Diplomacy*, No. 43, 2000.

> ➤ Like Chinese nuclear forces being designed to create first-strike uncertainty, the US multi-layered missile defence platforms could aggravate uncertainty for China, and reduce confidence on its retaliatory capabilities.

China's response to this threat envelope was the formulation of an active defence strategy which comprised of: (a) the numerical augmentation of its strike forces, including delivery vehicles and warheads so as to overwhelm strategic defences; (b) the extensive deployment of counter measures and decoys to neutralise interceptors which are susceptible to sensory distortions; (c) mount a diplomatic campaign against the militarisation of outer space to block space-based components of US missile defence; and (d) develop its own Anti Satellite (ASAT) and missile defence systems. While the first and second schemes are amply covered in the strategic modernisation effort, China was among the leading voices that supported the Prevention of Arms Race in Outer Space (PAROS), besides using various international forums to campaign against space weaponisation.[24] At a UN forum, a senior Chinese official said: "To pursue missile defence programs is part and parcel of the relevant country's long-term strategy to control outer space."[25] The dramatic shift in the Chinese approach was the decision taken to pursue development of ASAT and BMD capabilities, thus contradicting its vigorous campaigns against these very systems. Bao Shixiu, a PLA analyst, justifies this shift aptly.

---

24 On 12 February 2008, China and Russia presented at the Conference on Disarmament (CD) the joint draft of the "Treaty on the Prevention of the Placement of Weapons in Outer Space, the Threat or Use of Force against Outer Space Objects." Text available at: www.reachingcriticalwill.org/ political/cd/papers08/1session/Feb12%20Draft%20PPWT.pdf, accessed April 2013.

25 Fu Zhigang, "Concerns and Responses: A Chinese Perspective on NMD/ TMD," contributed paper to "Consultation on NATO Nuclear Policy, National Missile Defence& Alternative Security Arrangements," Ottawa, Canada, September 28–30, 2000, quoted by Pavel Podvig and Hui Zhang in *Russian and Chinese Responses to U.S. Military Plans in Space*, American Academy of Arts and Sciences, 2008, at http://belfercenter.ksg.harvard.edu/ files/militarySpace.pdf, accessed April 2013.

China is threatened by US policies in space, a reality that is compelling China to have its own space capabilities. A deterrent in space will decrease the possibility of the US attacking Chinese space assets... and will maintain the active defence strategy.[26]

This strategy, in fact, validates the predictions made by Alastair Johnston, who stated as early as 1995, that China will eventually develop these capabilities in its effort to attain limited deterrence.[27]

Chinese ASAT and BMD forays: In January 2007, Beijing sprang a surprise by testing its ASAT system, purportedly with a reconfigured version of DF-21C or DF-25.[28] Having acquired the capability for an outer-space interception, the expected next step was a ballistic missile interception, which it did through an exo-atmospheric test in January 2010.[29] Observers felt that the same platform used for the ASAT, termed as KS/SC-19, could have been used for the first BMD test, expectably with improved precision and kill capability. The Pentagon confirmed an exo-atmospheric interception, though the Chinese sought to create ambiguity by distributing photographs of its S-300 PMU after announcing the test. Exactly three years later, in January 2013, China undertook its second BMD test, though fewer details were released this time, thus adding to the speculation on whether a new system was tested. A handful of images and videos of an interception glare circulated on the Internet indicated the possibility of an endo-atmospheric interception which, if valid, points to the probable Chinese plan for multi-tier missile defence architecture, replicating the American model.[30] An endo-atmospheric interception using an

---

26 Remark in "Deterrence Revisited: Outer Space," *China Security*, Winter 2007.

27 See Johnston, n. 9.

28 Shirley Kan, "China's Anti-Satellite Weapon Test," *CRS Report for Congress*, 23 April 2007, http://www.fas.org/sgp/crs/row/RS22652.pdf, accessed April 2013.

29 For an assessment of the 2010 Chinese BMD test, see A. Vinod Kumar, "The Dragon's Shield: Intricacies of China's BMD Capability," *IDSA Issue Brief*, 25 February 2010.

30 A.Vinod Kumar, "Impressions on China's Second Missile Interceptor Test,"

S-300 PMU or any upgraded *Hongqi* versions may provide for a lower-tier interceptor in this plan. After a gap of 5 years, China conducted the third missile defence test in February 2018, which the official news agency claimed to be of the ground-based mid-course interceptor.[31] While some reports speculated this system to be the HQ-19—which actually is an air defence platform, and can at best be used for the endo-atmospheric interception instead of outer-space mid-course interception—some commentators also cited US officials as christening the system as *Dong Neng*-3 (DN-3/KO009).[32]

The active defence strategy also entails development of new kill-mediums, like a high-energy laser as well as high-powered microwave weapons for its ASAT.[33] While the USA ineluctably remains the primary focus of Chinese forays, the second interceptor test of 2013 was undertaken a little after India tested the *Agni*-V, which supposedly has the range to hit Beijing and larger parts of the Chinese hinterland. The development of *Agni*-V has enabled the progression of India's nuclear equation vis-à-vis China from a condition of existential deterrence to that of retaliatory deterrence, and also entails a challenge to the status quo created by the deployment of Chinese missiles in Tibet and Southern Military Regions. While the Chinese BMD will now have to include India's long-range missiles in its interception envelope, the complexity in this churning is the presence of India's own BMD platforms, which could impart the same kind of challenges that China confronts from the US BMD.

IDSA Strategic Comments, 22 February 2013.

31 "China conducts ground-based midcourse defence system test," *Peoples' Daily*, 6 February 2018, http://en.people.cn/n3/2018/0206/c90000-9424166. html, accessed February 2018.

32 Joseph Trevithick, "Let's talk about that mysterious Chinese anti-ballistic missile launch," *The Drive*, 6 February 2018, http://www.thedrive.com/ the-war-zone/18283/lets-talk-about-that-mysterious-chinese-anti-ballistic-missile-launch, accessed February 2018. Also see, Ankit Panda, "Revealed: The Details of China's Latest Hit-To-Kill Interceptor Test," *The Diplomat*, 21 February 2018.

33 See Pavel Podvig and Hui Zhang, n.25.

Thus, these developments buttress a multi-pronged Chinese strategy, which seems ongoing, and includes: (a) building a colossal offensive inventory for massive retaliation; (b) develop a nation-wide shield against long-range threats, and theatre defence against shorter-range ones; (c) deter India through southern deployments and project its missile defence capability against the *Agni*-V; (d) complicate the South Asian deterrence calculus by transferring its theatre defence platforms to Pakistan.

India: How far from credible minimum deterrence?

Among the many unique aspects of India's deterrence behaviour, a prominent characteristic is its intended design to provide a uniform posture of credible minimum deterrence against two nuclear rivals. In practice, though, India started out with the intention of developing a capability of existential deterrence against China (owing to the asymmetry) and retaliatory deterrence against Pakistan (also driven by a self-confidence of conventional forces superiority). The Indian quest towards attaining "credible minimum deterrence" since 1998 has been defined by the acquisition of various capabilities, chiefly a triad of delivery platforms aimed at establishing a survivable retaliatory nuclear force. Nearly two decades since the beginning of the overt nuclearisation phase, the Indian deterrent has progressed towards a multi-faceted dimension wherein a condition of retaliatory deterrence has perceptibly been established against China (with the development of *Agni* V) while the deterrence relationship with Pakistan is advancing from an existing state of retaliatory deterrence towards one of deterrence by denial (driven by the pursuit of a ballistic missile defence capability).

The second aspect is about the complex and volatile nature of the Southern Asian nuclear environment in which the Indian nuclear deterrent operates. Like China, whose strategic planning is influenced by the presence of multiple nuclear-armed actors in its strategic calculus, India practices its nuclear deterrence in two dyads: with China and Pakistan, both with widely different deterrence demands. As a result, it is often doubted if India's preference for a uniform deterrence template for both dyads could realistically fulfil its objectives; or rather, whether its current postures could provide credible and comprehensive deterrence for its immediate and extended threat environment. Though this demands a regular process of assessing and reinterpreting the extant of credibility and numerical strength of its deterrent and making suitable upgradations, there remains an irrefutable element of tentativeness and incertitude in India's postures when it comes to decisions about using nuclear weapons first, or invoking a uniform retaliatory posture for all scenarios, including those involving asymmetric threats and tactical weapons.

India is seeking to introduce its ballistic missile defence capability into this compact, with the inherent ambiguity on how it desires to recondition the deterrent environment with its BMD capability, or how it could posture this capability without altering its established deterrent structures. A basic analysis of India's nuclear deterrent has to touch upon a handful of overlapping areas: (a) the objectives of deterrence; (b) doctrinal structures; and (c) capabilities.

The Objective of deterrence: Similar to the Chinese deterrence model, India also pursues nuclear weapons for "self-defence" by propounding a "weaponised" route to nuclear disarmament which, though sounding paradoxical is primed on the strategic context of that era.[34] The draft nuclear doctrine (DND) exclaims: "In the absence of *global nuclear disarmament*, India's strategic interests require effective, credible nuclear deterrence and

---

34 Using Kanti Bajpai's description of three schools of thought in India's grand strategy formulation, namely Nehruvians, neo-liberals, and hyper-realists, the then National Security Advisor, Shiv Shankar Menon claimed in a lecture that all these three streams believe that nuclear weapons are essential for India's security in a world that has shown no signs of moving to their abolition and elimination—a statement that echoes the raisons d'être given in the DND for the nuclear weapons programme. See Kanti Bajpai, "India does do grand strategy," *Global Brief,* 5 March 2013, at *http://globalbrief.ca/ blog/2013/03/05/india-does-go-grand-strategy/*, accessed August 2017. Also see Shivshankar Menon, "The Role of Force in Strategic Affairs," Speech at National Defence College, 21 October 2010, at *http://www.mea.gov.in/ Speeches-Statements.htm?dtl/798/Speech+by+NSA+Shri+Shivshankar+M enon+at+NDC+on+The+Role+of+Force+in+Strategic+Affairs,* accessed December 2017.

adequate retaliatory capability ... this is consistent with the UN Charter, which sanctions the *right of self-defence*."[35] Endorsing that nuclear weapons are instruments of national and collective security, though only possessed by a few, India needs them "to deter the use and threat of use of nuclear weapons by any state or entity...." India also clarifies that it will not be the first to initiate a nuclear strike (NFU), and should deterrence fail, its retaliation with nuclear weapons will be massive and will inflict unacceptable damage.[36]

Thus, the basic essence of India's nuclear posture is that of a peace-loving country which, with its desire to defend itself against all possible threats, has opted to develop nuclear weapons after years of mastering the technology and yet abstaining from this pursuit in the hope of nuclear disarmament and total elimination. Owing to its non-offensive orientation, it is often argued that India perceives "deterrence as an instrument of politics and not as an operationalised strategic posture."[37] The primacy given to the political purpose instead of gaining a military advantage stems from the objectives sought through a "credible minimum deterrent", and conceptions about its strategic feasibility. For, votaries of the "minimum deterrence" argument contend that the primary goal of India's deterrent is to prevent any form of nuclear threat and blackmail which, in turn, also justifies the rationale of not using nuclear weapons except when subjected to a nuclear attack, and promising massive retaliation in return.[38] Accordingly, the Indian deterrent bases its credibility on the minimum number

---

35 See *Draft Report of National Security Advisory Board on Indian Nuclear Doctrine*, 17 August 1999, at http://www.mea.gov.in/in-focus-article.htm?18916/Draft+Report+of+National+Security+Advisory+Board+on+Indian+Nuclear+Doctrine, accessed August 2013.

36 Ibid. Also see, *Cabinet Committee on Security Reviews Progress in Operationalising India's Nuclear Doctrine*, 4 January 2003, at http://pib.nic.in/archieve/lreleng/lyr2003/rjan2003/04012003/r040120033.html, accessed August 2013.

37 Verghese Koithara, *Managing India's Nuclear Forces*, New Delhi: Routledge, 2012.

38 Shivshankar Menon, *Choices: Inside the Making of India's Foreign Policy*, Gurgaon: Penguin Random House, 2016.

of survivable forces that is assumed to be sufficient enough to impart unacceptable destruction on the adversaries, irrespective of the size of their arsenals or the posturing they will undertake through their arsenals.

A combination of factors, like global nuclear politics, the volatile security environment, and a perceived shift towards a realist grand strategy, prompted this nuclearisation path, though without seeking a tailor-made model that could reflect India's unique threat environment (of two nuclear-armed rivals) or providing for a flexible application of postures and doctrine to encompass the dual theatre. The luxury of emphasising a political mission instead of a war-fighting posture, though, remained limited to the initial years, with the expanding capabilities of India's adversaries putting stress on its own burgeoning inventory and doctrinal structures in the subsequent years. As a result, close to two decades after initiating this pursuit, India is visibly inching towards credible retaliatory capabilities for both dyads but still remains short of establishing (in comprehensive terms) what could amount to credible minimum deterrence, owing to the sustained push and pulls from a dynamic and ever-changing strategic milieu.

While nuclear doctrines are inherently about muscular sloganeering, the stated objectives in India's doctrine, even when being defensive in posture, leaves scope for scepticism on the scale of capabilities that are achievable (like the assured "survivability" of second strike forces, and the resilience of the political leadership following a devastating first strike), the tenability of declared postures (ability to stick to NFU when hostilities break out), or incredibly achieving what could be dependable "minimums" for both dyads. According to the DND, credibility is achieved "when the adversary knows that India can and will retaliate with sufficient nuclear weapons to inflict destruction and punishment that the aggressor will find unacceptable if nuclear weapons are used against India and its forces" (or a few other contingencies as subsequently qualified in various documents).[39] It remains a

---

39 The Cabinet Committee that operationalised the nuclear doctrine had expanded the conditionalities for nuclear use by stating that "India will (sic) retain the option of retaliating with nuclear weapons ... in the event

matter of conjecture on how much of the attainment of survivable forces for massive retaliation has been effectively signalled to India's adversaries in order for deterrence to take shape. While there might be greater appreciation among India's nuclear-armed rivals about the depth attained in its retaliatory capabilities, at least one party (Pakistan) has used the advances made in India's Triad as well as its non-weaponised nuclear infrastructure (like the Strategic Fuel Reserve facilitated by the India-US nuclear deal) as proof of India's expanding capabilities, and to justify the quantitative additions to its own nuclear and missile inventory.

Notwithstanding this contest, the vibrancy of India's nuclear deterrent invariably depends on how consistently and effectively India's security establishment (Executive Council of the National Command Authority, to be specific) constructs a realistic appreciation of the strategic environment and initiates real-time enhancements needed for the arsenal. For, rarely has there been debate in the public (or in informed) circles regarding what is entailed in the holistic whole in terms of a comprehensive deterrent capability, especially for each dyad, and whether "minimum" is the

---

of a major attack against India, or Indian forces anywhere, by biological or chemical weapons." See "Cabinet Committee on Security Reviews Progress in Operationalising India's Nuclear Doctrine," Press Release, Press Information Bureau, 4 January2003, available at:http://mea.gov.in/press-releases.htm?dtl/20131/The+Cabinet+Committee+on+Security+Reviews+perationalization+of+Indias+Nuclear+Doctrine, accessed February 2018. While the reference to "forces anywhere" in the DND and the Cabinet note could be assumed as including even enemy territory (proved relevant to the subsequent developments in the tactical nuclear theatre), the inclusion of biological and chemical weapons raised speculation about the potential for further revisions in the doctrinal framework in the coming years. A precursor to such possibilities was the debate ignited after a speech in 2010, by then National Security Adviser, Shivshankar Menon, at the National Defence College, New Delhi, during which he had referred to "no-first-use against non-nuclear weapons states," which many observers inferred as a significant doctrinal shift. Though it seemed a oratory slip with the probable reference being to a Cabinet note's line about "non-use of nuclear weapons against non-weapon states," Menon went on to mention the following in his book: "Some say that our declaration is meaningless as it is only a pious hope and does not cover other NWS." See "Choices", n.38 and "The Role of Force in Strategic Affairs," n. 34.

appropriate goal that India should aim at in the light of strategic advances by its rivals. Though quantifications of "minimum" and "limited" are contingent to individual national perceptions, the fact that China pursues a capability to deter the USA, and also that the Pakistani arsenal has advanced at a feverish pace could aggravate the security dilemma for India with regularity, and cause the shifting of goal posts. Thus, the current course of capability development leading towards the Triad remains a dynamic exercise, with the postural structures and capability assessments having to go through periodic transformations in order to address the evolving threat matrix. The DND addresses this requirement by stating that:

> This (credible minimum deterrence) is a dynamic concept related to the strategic environment, technological imperatives and the needs of national security. The actual size components, deployment, and employment of nuclear forces will be decided in the light of these factors...India's nuclear forces will be effective, enduring, diverse, flexible, and responsive to the requirements in accordance with the concept of credible minimum deterrence.

Doctrinal and postural structures: The core of India's nuclear doctrine is the no-first-use (NFU) posture, which reflects India's moralistic ethos of a peaceful nation. Nonetheless, it is this component of the doctrine that has been constantly criticised for its lack of realism or untenability. The foremost criticism is that India's NFU is inconsistent with the threat environment which is denoted by two nuclear-armed rivals with two different postures. Will a doctrine be potent if it equates with only one of the nuclear rivals, and creates a vacuum for the other to exploit? Pakistan is seen to have benefited from the resultant asymmetry by running a prolonged low-intensity conflict (LIC) against India, and consistently managing to deny the space for an Indian response by threatening to escalate to nuclear use. Though a nuclear overhang emerged in South Asia since the late 1980s—in a period termed as a covert nuclearisation phase—the propensity for escalation aggravated after 1998 when instances of sub-conventional confrontations caused major stand-offs, with the potential to spiral into full-fledged wars and nuclear conflagrations.[40] It was assumed that Pakistan carved out a space for LIC (initially as insurgency in Kashmir and, subsequently, through terror attacks across India) due to the vacuum created by India's NFU as Pakistan had refused to be drawn into a no-first-use equation and, instead, threatened to use nuclear weapons if India crossed any of its thresholds, which though were kept ambiguous.[41]

---

40 The two major crises in the covert nuclearisation phase were in 1987 and 1990. The 1987 crisis was a result of the Brasstacks exercise conducted by India in the Rajasthan desert, which Pakistan misread as battle preparation, prompting Gen. Zia ul Haq to make the first expression of a nuclear threat, and threshold when he told a magazine that "if they cross the border by an inch, their cities will be annihilated." For a glimpse of this episode, see Stephen Weisman, "On India's Border: A Huge Mock War," *The New York Times*, 6 March 1987. The 1990 crisis erupted over insurgency in Kashmir which was de-escalated after US intervention through the Robert Gates mission. See, Siddharth Varadarajan, "When Robert M. Gates Came Calling," *The Hindu*, 10 November 2006. The fears of South Asia as a nuclear flashpoint emerged soon after the 1998 nuclear tests when Indian and Pakistani armies had a limited conventional war in Kargil during which Pakistan issued numerous nuclear threats should Indian forces crossed the border. Following an attack on the Indian parliament in December 2001 by terrorist groups emanating from Pakistan, the Indian army mobilised forces along the border in a campaign termed 'Operation Parakram', which was defused after international intervention. The fifth crisis was after the terror attack in Mumbai in November 2008, which also saw international efforts for de-escalation. For a holistic analyses on the first four crises and their nuclear dimensions, See P. R. Chari, Pervaiz Iqbal Cheema, Stephen P. Cohen, *Four Crises and a Peace Process: American Engagement in South Asia*, Washington DC: Brooking Institution Press, 2007.

41 Pakistan had abstained from issuing a nuclear doctrine but had repeatedly conveyed its intention to use nuclear weapons first by arguing that India had conventional superiority. Since 1998, there have been numerous semi-official elucidations from Pakistan's personalities about redlines for its nuclear use, with some suggesting the crossing of the border by Indian forces and others suggesting an attack on a major Pakistani city or naval embargo or economic strangulation among potential thresholds. By far, the most credible articulation is assumed to be the one made by Lt. Gen. Khalid Kidwai (a long time head of Pakistan's Strategic Plans Division (SPD)), who said in an interview to an Italian institution, that the survival of Pakistani state should be seen as the most sensible threshold for Pakistan's nuclear response. See Paolo Cotta-Ramusino and Maurizio Martellini, "Nuclear Safety, Nuclear

While deterrence optimists termed this as a classic case of stability-instability paradox wherein conflict occurs at the lower level of the escalation ladder while stability prevails at the higher (nuclear) level, pessimists termed the South Asian case as an example of deterrence instability, with potential for regular face-offs and escalation potential.[42] Though many voices in India demanded a review of the NFU posture to correct this imbalance, some sections of the Indian leadership talked about exploring the space for limited war under a nuclear overhang.[43] With the apparent disadvantage prevailing for more than a decade after overt nuclearisation, the pursuit of new game-plans for military responses to the LIC—like the supposed Cold Start strategy (based on mobilisation shortcomings seen during Operation Parakram)[44]

Stability and Nuclear Strategy in Pakistan," Concise Report of a Visit by Landau Network - Centro Volta, 21 January 2002 (no Internet link currently available). Over the years, Pakistani officials have talked about a high threshold for using nuclear weapons while also indicating that nuclear use will be the 'last resort' under 'unthinkable' conditions.

42 See, E. Sridharan (ed.), *The India-Pakistan Nuclear Relationship*, New Delhi: Routledge, New Delhi, 2007; Sumit Ganguly, "Indo-Pakistani Nuclear Issues and the Stability/Instability Paradox," *Studies in Conflict and Terrorism*, Vol.18, 1995.

43 C. Raja Mohan, "Fernandes unveils 'limited war' doctrine," *The Hindu*, 24 January 2000.

44 The Cold Start strategy, supposedly devised by Indian Army's Shimla-based Training Command, was supposed to be the Army's attempt to carve a space for limited conventional responses to Pakistan-aided LIC without hitting its perceived nuclear thresholds. The strategy reportedly involved the reorganizing of the three strike corps into eight integrated battle groups (involving air and naval elements as well) that will launch multiple attacks on Pakistan territory (including terror camps and Pakistani strike corps assets) even as a holding corps will act as pivot force, and give defensive support and hold captured territory without hitting the supposed redlines that could trigger a nuclear action. Though the government has refused to endorse the existence of this strategy, Army officials involved in this exercise insist that the supposed 'Cold Start' is part of a handful of pro-active tactical plans that will be employed if the political leadership decides to undertake military action in response to a terror strike. At the height of this debate, Pakistan responded by projecting a tactical nuclear capability (*NASR*) with the declared intention to target Indian forces crossing into Pakistan territory. For a detailed analysis of Cold Start, see Walter C. Ladwig III, "A Cold Start

and the Surgical Strikes of September 2016[45] (following a terror attack in Uri Army camp)—demonstrated the willingness of India's political leadership to explore this space without hitting the presumed redlines or revising its doctrinal postures.

The India-China dyad, on the other hand, has seen comparatively greater stability despite a prolonged border dispute which has led to numerous skirmishes but sans a nuclear shadow. While it was the fledging Chinese nuclear programme that was among the factors supposed to have propelled the Indian peaceful nuclear explosion (PNE) of May 1974, the presence of an active proliferation corridor between China and Pakistan is assumed to have hastened the progress towards India's covert nuclearisation decision in the 1980s. The Chinese nuclear programme, which was surging until the 1990s, could also be listed as a major catalyst for India's decision to reject the Comprehensive Test Ban Treaty in 1995. Yet, the India-China nuclear relationship, especially after the formalisation of India's deterrence posture, remains a standing example of NFU as a stabiliser, even if that might be so largely in an equation where NFU is a uniform posture of both parties. The Doklam episode of 2017, when Chinese and Indian troops had a two-month standoff over a disputed territory, was an example of how the two nuclear-armed states had abstained from escalating the crisis to military hostilities.[46] Further, the "equaliser effect" of NFU in the India-China nuclear relationship also needs emphasis, considering the enduring conventional and nuclear force asymmetries notwithstanding India's attainment of retaliatory deterrence against China with its *Agni*-V system.

---

for Hot Wars? The Indian Army's New Limited War Doctrine," *International Security*, Vol. 32, No. 3, Winter 2007/08.

45 Surender Singh, "This is How 19 Indian Soldiers Did Surgical Strike in PoK, And Avenged the Uri Terror Attack," *India Times*, 9 February 2017, at https://www.indiatimes.com/news/india/this-is-how-19-indian-soldiers-did-surgical-strike-in-pok-and-avenged-the-uri-terror-attack-271166.html, accessed February 2018.

46 For an analysis, see A. Vinod Kumar, "Two Standoffs and Some Nuclear Lesson," *IDSA Strategic Comment*, 29 December 2017.

The second aspect is about the tenability of NFU as a dependable posture in actual conflict situations. Critics contend that India has restricted its options by confining itself to an NFU, especially the flexibility to pre-empt a potential first-strike.[47] On the other hand, many observers feel that India's NFU posture is merely declaratory and that it will exercise all options, including a pre-emptive first strike, in the event of credible intelligence of a potential nuclear strike. Questions are constantly raised on whether the Indian political leadership will be prepared to accept the cost of suffering the first strike, and whether they would accept the massive destruction of population centres in a nuclear attack or strategic assets. In fact, there are few tangible public articulations on how India will prepare itself for a nuclear strike or capability to absorb a first strike—be it about the consequence management from mass destruction of urban centres, safeguarding the political leadership (some references to bunkers), or the survivability of second strike forces, including the delegation of command and control to field commanders, and so on.

Many Indian commentators, including sceptics of the technology, have come around to the imperative of a missile defence shield in order to defend against a first blow (howsoever its efficacy), which could limit the devastation on the territory, population, as well as on second-strike capabilities.[48] On the other hand, the inconsistency in the NFU posture has also been berated, especially by foreign scholars. The shift from the DND's position that nuclear weapons will not be used against non-nuclear states, to the inclusion of the biological and chemical conditionality in the 2003 press release, and some subsequent articulations including the one attributed to the former NSA, are cited as examples of such wavering, also pointing to the certainty of NFU becoming irrelevant in realistic threat scenarios. Though such amendments and articulations are integral to the policy realignments in sync

---

47 Rajesh Rajagopalan, *Second Strike*: *Arguments about Nuclear war in South Asia*, New Delhi: Viking Penguin, 2005.

48 B.S. Nagal, "Checks and Balances," *Force*, June 2014.

with changing strategic scenarios,[49] the doctrine is still seen to be short on scenarios like tactical nuclear weapons or retaliatory options like counter-force.[50]

Some sections have demanded a doctrinal review, including the possibility of invoking new conditionalities in the NFU posture or making it theatre-specific.[51] It is also contended that a change of current policy to one of postural ambiguity could suit India's unique threat environment.[52] Though the government has consistently maintained the sacrosanct nature of the nuclear doctrine, the willingness to initiate postural realignments (as seen in the case of Cold Start) could be viewed as a lateral endorsement by the security establishment of the deficiencies in the postural structures as the threat matrix evolves. In fact, there are reasons to assume that the scope for postural revisions is being considered in a nuanced manner, either through signalling of new approaches (such as the emphasis given to massive retaliation by Shyam Saran), exploring new operational frameworks (like the Cold

---

49 P. R. Chari lists the intricacies in the preparation of the nuclear doctrine. See, "India's Nuclear Doctrine: Confused Ambitions," *The Non-Proliferation Review*, Fall-Winter 2000.

50 Koithara, n. 37.

51 In an unpublished paper titled "Low Intensity Conflict under Nuclear Conditions," presented at IDSA in 2009, I had proposed the need for theatre-specific posturing or regular signalling so as to convince the adversary about resolute operational flexibility within existing doctrinal structures or even the scope for their re-calibration if national security demands so. This approach was essential to ensure any doctrinal asymmetry or vacuum is not exploited; nor would the adversary be allowed to pursue political gains through nuclear brinkmanship.

52 Nagal, n. 48. It is also worth noting that the Bharatiya Janata Party (BJP), which is currently in power, had in its 2014 election manifesto, referred to the need to "study in detail India's nuclear doctrine, and revise and update it, to make it relevant to challenges of current times." Following speculation that the BJP could revise the doctrine, including the NFU clause, if voted to power, the party's top leadership stepped in to clarify that the NFU is sacrosanct. But it did not expound the dogmatic underpinnings behind its promise of an "independent strategic nuclear programme." In its four years in power since 2014, the BJP-led National Democratic Alliance (NDA) government has not initiated any postural review or discussions in this direction.

Start), or even pursuing space within the existing doctrinal matrix (such as surgical strikes).

Notwithstanding this nuanced approach, one cannot deny the certitude of constant postural reviews; this is so not just because of the changing contours of the threat environment, but also because of the fact that technological additions like BMD have not been accounted for in the current doctrinal framework. Moreover, the fact that India has been subjected to constant nuclear blackmail from Pakistan (reportedly around 17 times during the crises in Kargil and after the Parliament attack)—an aspect the credible minimum deterrent was meant to address—is an inherent factor that could fundamentally justify a doctrinal review.

The third aspect is about the credibility of the massive retaliation posture. While massive retaliation was seen as an appropriate posture for an NFU-oriented doctrine which relies on second-strike and retaliatory deterrence, there are standard doubts associated with this principle as the deterrence scene evolves. First, given its current technological pace that India can afford, can it realistically attain the capability of massive retaliation against China, which could imply endowing unacceptable damage to counter-value and counter-force assets within that huge territorial landmass? Second, can India convincingly secure its retaliatory capability in the event of a first strike, and invigorate its command and control systems to initiate a devastating massive retaliation on multiple theatres? The third issue is about India's response to a tactical strike by Pakistan using its *Nasr* system, which is particularly conceived as a probable scenario of an attack on India's integrated battle groups or strike corps advancing into Pakistan territory. India has signalled (through Shyam Saran's statements as Chairman of the National Security Advisory Board) that it does not differentiate between a tactical or strategic attack, implying that any first-use will attract a massive retaliation.[53]

---

53 Shyam Saran clarified the Indian approach towards strategic and tactical weapons in a lecture on 24 April 2013, titled: "Is India's Nuclear Deterrent Credible?" Text available at: http://ris.org.in/images/RIS_images/pdf/ Final%20Is%20India's%20Nuclear%20Deterrent%20Credible-%20 rev1%202%202.pdf, accessed April 2013. Also see, Shyam Saran, "Weapon

However, many observers criticize this posture as being bellicose and inherently escalatory, though, for the Indian security establishment, it implies the refusal to open space for a tactical nuclear theatre. On the other hand, various sections have demanded a similar technological riposte from India, which could enable a nuclear warfighting capability at the tactical level. Though an Indian delivery system for tactical nuclear warheads (*Prahaar*)[54] is known to be under development, many voices warn against pushing for a tactical envelope as it involves delegating the command and control of nuclear weapons to battlefield commanders, with no guarantee against its further escalation or an all-out nuclear war.[55] While an Indian multi-pronged response to the *Nasr* challenge—emphasising the massive retaliation posture, *Prahaar* and missile defence—could have been relatively effective in correcting the perceived postural imbalance, it is widely felt that India should re-tailor its retaliatory options and postures for such theatre scenarios.

When holistically assessed, India's deterrence posture unwittingly projects the improbability of a nuclear war, though not its inevitability, assuming that the eventual act of "massive retaliation" will be for a "final battle" using all strategic resources beyond which the situation cannot be reasonably imagined. There are fewer indications that a nuclear war-fighting strategy or the scope of limited nuclear wars has been considered in

---

that has more than symbolic value," *The Hindu*, 4 May 2013.

54 The range of this system is believed to be 150–300 km. While various reports indicate *Prahaar*'s development since 2011, former Defence Research and Development Organisation (DRDO) chief, Dr. V.K. Saraswat, had confirmed its ongoing development in a presentation delivered at IDSA in February 2017. He, however, refused to confirm whether it will be a tactical nuclear delivery capability like, or as a response to, Pakistan's *Nasr* system. It seems the Indian security establishment is not currently considering any projection of a tactical nuclear capability. For an analysis about *Prahaar*, see "USA's MGM-140 ATACMS vs. India's *Prahaar* vs. Pakistan's *Nasr*, Tactical Ballistic Missile Comparison," 10 January 2016, at http://aermech.in/usas-mgm-140-atacms-vs-indias-*Prahaar*-vs-pakistans-*Nasr*-tactical-ballistic-missile-comparison/, accessed February 2018.

55 Nagal, n. 48.

the doctrinal planning. Similarly, despite survivability being a cardinal principle, and work on the Triad (with the submarine force being the survivable leg) progressing at a considerable pace, there remains a cloud of ambiguity (or a public reassurance) on whether the Indian leadership will recover from the massive loss of population centres in the event of a formidable first strike, or whether the leadership and security establishment are realistically prepared for such eventualities. The relevance of a nation-wide missile defence shield emerges in this context as a substantive pillar of deterrence that needs incorporation through a doctrinal realignment.

Capabilities: India has not been in a position to project credible minimum deterrence because many of the requisite capabilities, essentially the "survivable" naval leg of the triad, are still evolving or at advanced stages of development (see Preface for latest update). Thus, there are two factors that impinge on the progress towards this objective, howsoever dynamic it may remain. First, the time needed to deploy a "survivable" triad of retaliatory platforms; and second, deciding whether a designated number of platforms will be sufficient to create credible minimum deterrence. Though many of the delivery platforms, including the *Prithvi* and *Agni* variants, have been in development since the 1980s as part of the Integrated Guided Missile Development Programme (IGMDP), and work on warheads has been ongoing since the 1970s, the delay in achieving the triad close to two decades after overt nuclearisation places immense pressure on the ability of the security establishment to credibly project comprehensive deterrence on the two dynamic dyads.

While sufficient headway has been achieved in recent years on land-based delivery systems, the naval leg has faced numerous delays, which includes the dual challenges of developing nuclear-powered submarines as also developing and integrating submarine-launched ballistic missile (SLBMs) for shorter and longer ranges for the dyadic requirements.[56] In recent months, major milestones

---

56 For a detailed survey of capabilities, see AjeyLele and Praveen Bhardwaj, "India's Nuclear Triad: A Net Assessment," *IDSA Occasional Paper No.31*, April 2013, at: http://idsa.in/system/files/OP_IndiasNuclearTriad.pdf,

have been achieved on the *Sagarika* and *Dhanush* SLBMs as also the *Arihant* nuclear submarine. However, it will take many more months before their operational deployment. On the other hand, two variants of the *Prithvi* (I & II), its naval variant (*Dhanush*)—all with definite coverage over Pakistan—and three variants of the *Agni* series (I, II and III)—which endow short- to medium-range coverage over China (especially targets in the Southern Military Region)—have supposedly been inducted, and are regularly tested by the Strategic Forces Command (SFC) which has operational control over the deterrent assets. The longer-range versions of *Agni* (mainly IV and V variants), intended to provide retaliatory deterrence against China, are still under development amid talk of an inter-continental ballistic missile (ICBM) also being currently under development with India's Defence Research Development Organisation (DRDO).[57] Similarly, of the naval variants that could form the survivable components—the K-15 at 700 km and K-4 at 3000 km ranges—are supposedly in advanced stages of development even as the probability for a longer-range SLBM that could provide survivable retaliatory capability against China (the K-5 at 6000 km) is rumoured to be in the works. At the other end, it is presumed that warheads based on boosted-fission devices are deployed amid speculations on the thermonuclear device.[58]

---

accessed March 2015.

57 Some reports dub this as *Agni*-VI (Surya) at around 8000–12,000 km range, though it is unclear why India will seek an ICBM capability when its farthest challenge will only be to target counter-value assets in China that are within the 5000 km radius. For a debate, see A. Vinod Kumar, "Does India need ICBMs?" *Bulletin of the Atomic Scientists*, 10 May 2012. Also see, Vikas, "Is India developing a 12,000 kms range missile: Surya?" *One India*, 17 November 2017, at: https://www.drdo.gov.in/drdo/pub/npc/2017/november/din-17november2017.pdf, accessed February 2018. In a presentation at IDSA in February 2017, former DRDO chief, V. K. Saraswat confirmed the plans to develop *Agni*-VI, but did not elaborate on its details.

58 Since the 1998 tests, the scientific and strategic communities have been divided on the yield of the thermonuclear device. However, a former chief of DAE told this author that, apart from a satisfactory yield, the thermonuclear device has already been deployed, though the veracity of this claim cannot be confirmed yet.

The other issue is about determining if the evolving triad will be sufficient to provide credible minimum deterrence. This has become relevant considering the rapid advances made by the two nuclear adversaries. Pakistan's effort to match India's capabilities has been constantly pushing the envelope for India; even as India's effort to square the asymmetry with China remains a pressure point owing to its strategic modernisation programme. Both cause the shifting of goalposts for India. The development of *Agni-V* and inroads in BMD technology are significant breakthroughs that bring the combined characteristics of both punitive and denial deterrence to the Southern Asian nuclear theatre, though it is still too early to infer whether they will bring deterrence stability or vitiate the equations. The finality of minimum deterrence will be determined by numerous other factors, most important being the confirmation of a "survivable" triad. For this purpose, India needs to project its capabilities in mobility, well-concealed silos or underground storage facilities, the wherewithal to absorb a first-strike, the ability for instant retaliation through attributes like launch-on-warning and effective command and control, among others, as conceived by the DND. There is painfully little information on the progress of these components, though some analysts hint at significant headway based on selective official briefings.[59] However, until these capabilities seem dependable to the leadership or in public perception, projecting credible minimum deterrence may be difficult. Further, scenarios of retaliation, including counter-force, counter-military, and counter-value, as well as involving tactical nuclear weapons, need to be considered in their entirety before the credibility index of the deterrent is pronounced.

India's Missile Defence Strategy

Explanations on why India needs missile defence will be similar to the rationale that drives China's BMD aspirations. Unlike China though, India has not been critical of the US missile defence programme, and had rather initiated its pursuit around the same

---

59 See, Bharat Karnad, *India's Nuclear Policy*, Westport, Connecticut: Praeger Security International, 2008.

time it decided in favour of publicising its deterrent. According to available literature, the programme was conceived in the late 1990s, following the transfer of Chinese M-9 and M-11 missiles to Pakistan as part of the proliferation channel that was active during the 1980s. Pakistan's brinkmanship behaviour during the two crises between the 1998 tests and the formalisation of the Indian doctrine in 2003 convinced Indian leaders about the NFU posture being exploited, and the denial of space for a response to sub-conventional campaigns. The need to call Pakistan's "nuclear bluff", and deny it any scope of first-use are assumed to be among the foremost strategic drivers that have since buttressed India's missile defence effort, with ample support from the political leadership. Yet, India's programme cannot be termed as Pakistan-centric, but as a holistic shield from both Pakistani and Chinese missiles, especially since the vulnerability to Chinese missile systems has been a perennial strategic challenge.

Going by the progress of the BMD programme since the first test of an interceptor in 2006, at least two broad factors can be identified as the current catalyst for the programme.

➤ India's missile defence programme could be seen as part of the two-pronged strategy (the other being Cold Start or a proactive military plan) to curtail opportunities for Pakistan to exploit India's NFU, and inhibit its responses to the LIC with the threat of nuclear use. India could aspire to use its missile defence to intercept or limit damage from a first-strike and undertake massive retaliation, thus neutralising the Pakistani capability, and render its deterrent effete. If this plan is workable as conceived, the Indian missile defence platforms could alter the deterrence status quo while sustaining its NFU posture, and also limiting Pakistan options of escalation. The costs are higher for Pakistan, considering that even an intercepted first-strike could invite retaliation, and a massive one at that, going by current posturing.

➤ The missile defence matrix with China, on the other hand, will be multi-faceted. India seeks to develop longer-range mid-course interception platforms, with the goal of intercepting Chinese missiles deployed in its Southern Military Region. When projected in unison with the *Agni*-V (with the capability to hit Beijing), a mid-course interception capability will provide India with greater defensive and deterrence depth, and could impart credibility to the Indian deterrent vis-à-vis China, whether projected as minimum or limited. However, considering that China is also developing missile defences and could use the same strategy against Indian forces, the scope for defensive parity emerges in the dyad which might, in the long run, provide for a stable deterrence equation or even an equalizer effect.

The Indian missile defence programme was a closely-guarded secret until 2006 when the DRDO first undertook the *Prithvi* Air Defence Experiment (PADE). Maintaining secrecy for over a decade is puzzling, considering that nations developing strategic interceptors have sought to project this capability from the early stages of development itself so as to put their rivals on notice. One probable reason could be the uncertainty about developing such high-end technology whose global success rate has been, and continues to remain, low, with the successful interceptions undertaken even by advanced military powers being done in simulated conditions (the US GMDs being a prominent example). It certainly surprised observers that the first PADE test in November 2006 was declared a successful endo-atmospheric interception. Subsequently, DRDO announced a multi-layer architectural plan, with the *Prithvi* Air Defence (PAD) system for the upper tier or for area defence, and the Advanced Air Defence (AAD) system for the lower tier or point defence.

A handful of development tests were undertaken on both systems, with a remarkably high rate of success. While the PAD has interception coverage against missiles with 1000–2000 km range at altitudes of 50–80 km, the AAD system covers shorter-range missiles, with interception altitudes of 15–30 km. Despite both being essentially endo-atmospheric interceptors (below the 100 km altitude), the DRDO projected the PAD as an exo-atmospheric interceptor, with its own definition of range.[60] Nonetheless, using the high-rate of successful interceptions in the initial testing series till around the 2012–13 period, the DRDO decided to declare the system operational, and ready for deployment to protect the National Capital Region.[61] However, the political leadership did not seem convinced on the demonstrated capability, as evident from the lack of enthusiasm in favour of a rapid deployment plan. At the core of such indecision will be the reluctance to place all bets on a technological concept that is yet to be deemed foolproof, especially when the stakes involve a nuclear conflagration and holocaustic outcomes.

With its current range, the PAD is supposed to be capable of targeting Pakistani systems like the *Ghauri-I* and *Shaheen-II* (under the 1500 km range) and, in principle, provide extended area defence to major parts of northern India, depending on the deployment pattern. However, to endow a nation-wide coverage against longer-range and faster Chinese and Pakistani missiles, India has to develop an exo-atmospheric system which could target incoming missiles with over 3500–5000 km range, at an interception altitude of 120–150 km. This quest is currently being pursued through the AD (PDV)-1&2 systems, though the effort was initially reported to be handicapped by the absence of suitable long-range tracking radars (LRTRs). Currently, India uses the 600 km range Greenpine radar to support the PAD system, which has largely used the *Prithvi* missiles as targets.[62] For the exo-atmospheric tests, the DRDO had begun trials with *Agni* systems as targets, though the success of this platform will be directly linked to the capability for long-range tracking, and the successful interception outside the Earth's atmosphere where gravitational

---

60 When the author raised this query with a senior DRDO official associated with the BMD programme, his reply was, "each country defines its own range as either endo- or exo-atmosphere."

61 "Missile Defence System Ready for Induction: DRDO Chief," *The Indian Express*, 21 March 2013.

62 While it was known that the DRDO and the Indian Air Force have been working with Israeli and French companies to plug this gap, officials privy to this process recently indicated to the author that the range of this radar system has been enhanced to complement the long range interceptor.

dynamics will be different from that of the endo-atmosphere. The first test of the PDV-1 to attain interception at a range of 120 km was conducted in April 2014.[63] Though the DRDO claimed the mission was successful (in terms of inertial guidance and target seeking), the launch could not achieve a successful interception.[64] While the second PDV test in February 2017 was reported as a success, the DRDO seems to be exercising visible caution by abstaining from a tight test schedule for the PDV, of declaring early success, as done in the case of PAD and AAD projects.[65]

Interestingly, neither the political leadership nor the security establishment has articulated their vision of a missile defence shield or its strategic dimensions. Do they envision a nation-wide shield, and rely on its ability for the comprehensive defence of the homeland? Do they believe that the existing doctrinal structures need to be revised to project a posture of denial deterrence? Or, do they envisage an aggressive deterrent posture with missile defence adding to the net offensive capability, et al? But regarding the DRDO's claims of "successful" test and the potential capabilities of the systems being developed, there seems to be little debate of substance or a national discourse on whether a limited missile defence shield will serve India's purpose, or whether a nation-wide coverage should be considered as a feasible option. With a deployment architecture that facilitates overlapping coverage, the PAD-AAD combine could provide a modest-to-accurate point as well as area defence against short and medium range missiles emanating from Pakistan and China. However, for the longer range missiles (especially the Chinese) that could reach the Indian heartland and strategic assets located down the northern frontier (which Pakistan's *Shaheen III* also intends to target), a longer-range

---

63 Hemant Kumar Rout, *"Prithvi* Defence Vehicle Fails to Intercept," *New Indian Express*, 15 May 2014.

64 See DRDO press release, at: http://www.drdo.gov.in/drdo/English/dpi/press_release/pdv.pdf, accessed May 2014. A senior DRDO official later confirmed to this author that the interception could not be achieved, and that more tests have to be conducted on the PDV before declaring it fit for deployment.

65 "India successfully test-fires interceptor missile off Odisha coast," *Press Trust of India*, 11 February 2017.

interceptor (that could do mid-course interception) in wider and dispersed deployment is vital to achieving nation-wide coverage. The success of PDV, along with the deployment of a wide array of surveillance and tracking systems—including radars and satellite systems—remains at the heart of attaining nation-wide coverage, be it in modest terms or for large-scale deployment (in order to cover both dyads and aspire to transform the deterrence matrix). Similarly, there is a different set of challenges that cloud the lower end of the spectrum where the AAD system is supposed to provide point defence (along with existing surface-to-air missiles) but may still find the theatre challenging when subjected to below-the-radar air-breathing threats, like cruise missiles, in both air-launched and land-attack versions.

As India's political and military leaderships deliberate on the role and space for missile defence in the country's nuclear strategy, formulating a doctrinal framework to define its employment remains a key imperative. This could include incorporating the role and objectives of the missile defence in a revised nuclear doctrine that could integrate the space for denial deterrence (alongside retaliation) in India's posture or even convey to the adversary India's intention to deny space for a nuclear attack (either first-use or in retaliation). Essentially, such a revision could innately project the country's acquisition of a net deterrence value with the integration of defensive depth with retaliatory forces. Though a doctrinal revision for this purpose cannot be immediately foreseen, there is scope for an initial operational framework to define agency roles and structures, and carving out the functional position in the strategic arsenal.

Currently, the Indian Air Force (IAF) has operational control over the programme in order to facilitate an integrated air and missile defence network against all air-breathing and missile threats. However, if the missile defence systems are intended to complement the minimum deterrent, then it should ideally be taking on a strategic character by switching operational control to the Strategic Forces Command (SFC), which is the custodian of India's nuclear forces. Though no such thinking currently seems to be under consideration, they may come into play when the deterrent roles of BMD are identified by the government, and also when India explores the option of a naval interceptor (which might be operated by the Indian Navy instead of the IAF). Even though there is no notable discussion on a potential naval interceptor, the possibility of India acquiring the Standard Missile (SM-3/6) as a naval variant at some stage from the USA cannot be completely ruled out, especially if the political leadership feels the need for a system that could provide for late descent/early ascent or boost-phase interception against Pakistani missiles.

The Indo-US Next Step in Strategic Partnership (NSSP) of 2004 had, for that matter, enshrined the possibility of cooperation in missile defences, though this effort has been stymied by DRDO's purported resistance to external inputs in the BMD programme. Yet, if the agency faces difficulties in developing a credible exo-atmospheric interceptor, the possibility of acquiring American systems may inherently open up. Interestingly, India had earlier sought the *Arrow* system from Israel and the USA. Despite Israel's keenness, Washington had refused to part with the *Arrow* and had, instead, offered the PAC-3. India declined this offer as the DRDO could have claimed the ability to develop the same spectrum of capabilities with its PAD and AAD platforms. Nonetheless, it may be difficult to rule out the possibility of American interceptors—including endo-atmospheric ones like THAAD—coming into the Indian inventory at some stage, especially if the political leadership seeks to strengthen the denial deterrence framework. On the other hand, since 2015 India was planning to acquire the Russian S-400 (*Trimuf*) system, which could provide both air defence and ballistic missile defence capabilities to the Indian forces.[66] This could be a precursor to a larger level of cooperation with the Russians in the area of missile defence, especially with their upcoming systems like S-500, as well as on long-range tracking capability. For, the IAF is known to have acquired the S-300 as a first response to

---

66 Recent updates about the S-400 acquisition and its strategic manifestations have been described in the Preface. Rajat Pandit, "India eyes safer skies with Russian S-400 *Triumf*," *Times of India*, 11 October 2015; "India to sign S-400 *Triumf* missile deal with Russia soon, says Nirmala Sitharaman; rejects US sanctions on Moscow," *First Post*, 14 July 2018.

the M-9 acquisition by Pakistan and could be open to integrating newer Russian platforms into an ecosystem that is used to Russian technology.

However, all such calculations are intrinsically linked to the DRDO's ability to develop a nation-wide architecture as well as the costs involved in this process, whose estimate, when last counted half a decade ago, was over INR17,000 crores. Considering that the DRDO had managed to drive a national mood in favour of missile defence, with very few questions raised in the public domain about its development claims despite its poor record on many other military technologies, the prospect of more financial support to this programme stands bright as things stand today. Further, the political class, and the military and strategic communities have also backed the strategic rationale for the missile defence programme, which has, in turn, enabled the DRDO to define its strategic dimensions and influence operational requirements.

Pakistan: Deterrence Challenged?

For a country that vowed to "eat grass" if it needed to make nuclear weapons, the creation of a burgeoning nuclear arsenal, backed by its aggressive deterrent posture to keep its arch rival at bay, symbolises the rare success of a "national interest" project amid other failures in nation-building. With its weak economic base, Pakistan considered nuclear deterrence as a great equalizer, and a cheaper route to offset India's conventional superiority[67] by using a combination of belligerent and ambiguous posturing and denying the space for any form of military responses from India to the threats or actions emanating from Pakistan. This policy has been justified as an imperative of national survival, though the actual political objective was invariably to change the status quo in the Kashmir dispute in its favour, and maybe, by some accounts, even check India's "hegemonic" rise in the region. Towards this end, Pakistan ran a prolonged low-intensity conflict in Indian territory,

67 Rasul Bakhsh Rais, "Conceptualizing Nuclear Deterrence: Pakistan's Posture," *India Review*, No. 4(2), 2005.

threatened rapid escalation, and used nuclear brinkmanship to attract international attention to the dispute and the region, which soon came to be described as a nuclear flashpoint.

This strategy saw a successful run in the early years of overt nuclearisation, until the 9/11 attacks changed the global narrative on terrorism, and began to impact this strategy. However, Pakistan continues to see virtue in it by the fact that India was deterred from any substantive cross-border responses, and has been forced to a composite dialogue process, irrespective of its being effete. Though Pakistan has constantly claimed minimum deterrence, strategic restraint, and nuclear stability as the core values of its nuclear programme, its grand strategy has always been about using nuclear weapons to derive benefits from instability and from the international focus on the region.[68] Many observers use the stability-instability paradox to justify this as an inherent nature of nuclear weapons, though in this dyad, it has by and large benefited Pakistan. Following three major standoffs in the overt nuclearisation period, India realised the need to alter the status quo through a series of strategic realignments which have included the conventional doctrinal shift (perceived as an attempt to open space for a limited conventional war), the introduction of missile defence as a means to challenge the postural gains that accrued to Pakistan, and the surgical strike of 2016 illustrating India's attempt to respond to the LIC below the imaginable nuclear thresholds.

While the major part of the two decades of nuclearisation in South Asia was witness to this race for gaining a deterrence upper hand, the last few years was more about Pakistan's desperate efforts to regain the lost advantage by pursuing changes in its postural structures and expanding capabilities, with the declared intention of establishing "full spectrum" deterrence. Though these actions could be seen as portraying the intensification of the strategic competition in this dyad, it also underlines the prospects

---

68 "Remarks by Prime Minister Nawaz Sharif on Nuclear Policies and the CTBT," National Defence College, Islamabad, 20 May 1999, quoted by Bhumitra Chakma, "Pakistan's Nuclear Doctrine and Command and Control System: Dilemmas of Small Nuclear Forces in the Second Atomic Age," *Security Challenges*, Vol. 2(2), July 2006.

of a stabilising impact with both nations finding lesser space to raise the tempo of conflict to higher escalatory thresholds. More importantly, the fact that the exogenous strategic environment is no longer favouring Pakistan has forced a notable shift in its nuclear behaviour in recent years. The increasing costs that Pakistan is bearing on the LIC, thanks to the international focus on its terror infrastructure, the political setbacks it conceives as accruing from India's mainstreaming through the India-US nuclear deal, the introduction of tactical nuclear capability not deriving the intended benefits, and the introduction of India's missile defence, etc., are factors that have forced Pakistan to recalibrate its nuclear structures in order to project itself as a "responsible nuclear-weapons state." The change in the calculus is most tangibly illustrated by the fact that Pakistan is currently projecting a second-strike capability along with flexible (or graduated) response options, after years of maintaining first strike options and displaying brinkmanship behaviour.[69]

Doctrinal and postural structures: Besides being India-centric and having the proclaimed objective of achieving credible minimum deterrence, Pakistan has, for long, reserved the option of using nuclear weapons first, irrespective of the nature of the military campaign it is subjected to. For this purpose, Pakistan has repeatedly highlighted two operational goals: (a) deter India at all the three levels of the spectrum—be it sub-conventional, conventional, or nuclear—which some analysts explain as "full-spectrum minimum deterrence," (minimalism of capability emphasized, and spectrum denoting the theatre); and (b) maintain ambiguous thresholds on nuclear use in order for deterrence to be effective.[70] However, the tenability of Pakistan's first-strike

---

69 Some observers also see the recent changes in capability and posture as an attempt to gain 'assured deterrence'. See Adil Sultan, "Pakistan's emerging nuclear posture: impact of drivers and technology on nuclear doctrine," *Strategic Studies*, http://issi.org.pk/strategic-studies-4/, accessed February 2018. Also see, Sadia Tasleem, "Pakistan's Nuclear Use Doctrine," *Carnegie Endowment for International Peace*, 30 June 2016, at http://carnegieendowment.org/2016/06/30/pakistan-s-nuclear-use-doctrine-pub-63913, accessed February 2018.

70 The term is used by Brig. Naeem Salik, a former Pakistani Army officer who

posture and its nuclear-use thresholds has been subjected to constant scrutiny. Pakistan is not known to have formally enshrined first-strike as a doctrine but has only rejected India's NFU as a ploy to exploit its conventional advantage and has also, through numerous articulations, declared the intention to retain the option of using nuclear weapons first.[71] It is often argued that first-strike is a natural and only choice, given its inherent weaknesses when it comes to conventional forces.[72] In many ways, it could also be seen as a posture to guarantee survival as few are confident that a first-strike posture will lead to a winnable nuclear war when the eventual outcome could be "unacceptable destruction" from massive Indian retaliation. Hence, more than a nuclear warfighting strategy, the offensive posturing seemed an initial pathway to pursue political objectives backed by the deliberate ambiguity of nuclear thresholds.

Indeed, ambiguity has remained at the core of Pakistan's nuclear posturing, with numerous redlines being signalled through semi-official declarations and threats. Starting with Zia ul Haq's statement during the Brasstacks crisis in 1987, Pakistani officials have, during various crises, constantly referred to the "undisputed border" as the territorial threshold which could trigger the "ultimate option."[73] Other inconsistent expositions of redlines include: the

served in Pakistan's Strategic Plans Division. The distinction in usage of 'full spectrum' is relevant when considering the current evolution of Pakistan's nuclear forces and posture. While full spectrum in the earlier context denoted the theatre, and emphasized the minimal nature of the deterrent, the current context is of capabilities ranging from conventional to tactical and strategic dimensions. See Naeem Salik, "Pakistan's Nuclear Force Structure in 2025," *Carnegie Endowment for International Peace*, 30 June 2016, at http://carnegieendowment.org/2016/06/30/pakistan-s-nuclear-force-structure-in-2025-pub-63912, accessed February 2018.

71 Mahmud Ali Durrani, "Pakistan's Strategic Thinking and the Role of Nuclear Weapons," Cooperative Monitoring Centre Occasional Paper, Sandia National Laboratories, July 2004.

72 Besides the inherently smaller army in terms of number compared to India, the short coastline and territory in comparison to India implies a smaller Navy and Air Force.

73 Kamran Khan, "PM-GHQ in harmony, to maintain status quo in Kargil," *The New International*, 24 June 1999. Also see, "Any weapons will be used,

penetration of Indian forces beyond a (defined) line or crossing of a river, the capture of an important Pakistani city, destruction beyond acceptable level of its conventional forces, attack on strategic assets, blockade of its vital supply lines, and even the crossing of the LoC that threatens Pakistan control over occupied Kashmir, among others.[74] While most of these articulations were dismissed as lacking credibility, it was the exposition given by Lieutenant General Khalid Kidwai, a long-time Chief of Pakistan's Strategic Plans Division (SPD), to an Italian institute in 2002 which was held as a credible definition of Pakistan's nuclear use threshold for a long time. In the exposition, Kidwai clarified the conditions that could prompt Pakistan to resort to nuclear use. These included (a) India attacking and conquering a large part of its territory; (b) destroying a large section of its land and air forces; (c) proceeding to the economic strangulation of Pakistan (implying a naval blockade of the Karachi port); and (d) pushing Pakistan into political destabilisation or creating large-scale internal subversion.[75]

While some of these thresholds, if taken singularly, may occur as an outcome of a major conventional war with India and hence may not warrant a total nuclear war, it is generally assumed that Pakistan will resort to a nuclear endgame only when its survival as a nation-state is in real jeopardy.[76] Owing to this eventuality, despite occasional projections about its capability (through frequent tests) and deterrence structures (full-spectrum), Pakistan feels that maintaining ambiguity about its doctrine and numbers should remain the core of its nuclear posture. Kidwai explained this policy recently thus: "Pakistan follows a policy of

threatens Pakistan," *The Hindu*, 1 June 1999.

74 Tariq Mahmud Ashraf, *Aerospace Power: The Emerging Strategic Dimension*, Peshawar: PAF Book Club, 2003.

75 See, Cotta-Ramusion, Paolo and Maurizio Martellini, n.41.

76 Michael Krepon, "Pakistan's Nuclear Strategy and Deterrence Stability," *Stimson Center*, 12 May 2012, at www.stimson.org/images/uploads/research-pdfs/Krepon-_Pakistan_Nuclear_Strategy_and_Deterrence_Stability.pdf, accessed August 2013.

ambiguity, in a very well deliberated and thought out manner. I don't think any government of Pakistan will want to abandon the policy of ambiguity."[77]

Capabilities: Besides a substantial air fleet comprising F-16 A/B and Mirage III/V aircraft (and potential conversion of Chinese-supplied JF-17 to nuclear-capability), Pakistan's nuclear deterrent is largely centred on the strategic missile force with varying ranges to cover the Indian sub-continent. It includes the short-range variety, comprising *Abdali/Hatf-2* (180 km), *Ghaznavi/ Hatf-3* (250 km), *Shaheen-1/Hatf-4* (750 km), and *Shaheen-1A/ Hatf-4* (900 km); and the medium range ones of *Shaheen-2/Hatf-6* (1500 km), and *Ghauri/Hatf-5* (1250 km).[78] The wide-ranging inventory denotes the capability to target numerous population centres and counter-force assets, ranging from those close to the border as also other parts of the northern heartland, including the National Capital Region. By dispersing its warheads and focusing on road-mobile launchers, Pakistan has made efforts to enhance the mobility and survivability of its forces, along with a military-centric command and control system and reported delegation to field commanders—all with the intention of enhancing the perceptions of credibility, both within and outside. A notable capability addition in recent years has been of the *Shaheen-3* (*Hatf-10*), with a projected range of around 2750 km. According to Kidwai, "2,750 km is a very well calculated range that provides comprehensive coverage of any particular land area [in which] India might think of putting its weapons."[79] Beyond targeting any missile or aircraft base in the Indian hinterland, the *Shaheen-3*, according to Kidwai, is intended to reach the Andaman and Nicobar Islands, which Pakistan thinks will be a strategic base for anchoring India's second strike capability.

At the other end of the spectrum are two significant streams

---

77 "A Conversation with Gen. Khalid Kidwai," *Monitor 360*, Carnegie International Nuclear Policy Conference 2015, 23 March 2015.

78 Hans M. Kristensen and Robert S. Norris, "Pakistani nuclear forces, 2016," *Bulletin of the Atomic Scientists*, 31 October 2016.

79 Kidwai, n.77.

of capability advancement that Pakistan has vigorously pursued, namely, the *Nasr/Hatf-9* at 60 km range as a tactical nuclear delivery system (intended to target forward moving Indian troops as part of any pro-active military strategy), and two cruise missile systems: the *Babur/Hatf-7* (land-attack) and the *Ra'ad/Hatf-8* (air-launched)—both of 350 km range, and with the desired objective of defeating the Indian missile defence systems. Complementing this sustained expansion of the missile inventory is the feverish augmentation of its fissile stocks, followed by reported efforts to build plutonium warheads along with uranium, and using its military ties with China to acquire new platforms. Yet, the most significant shift is the indicated plans to pursue a submarine-based "survivable" second-strike capability that could be used to convey a "massive retaliation" capability to deter any potential Indian pre-emption plans or spell potential for a final "revenge" war following a devastating massive retaliation to a Pakistani first strike.[80] Kidwai also rationalizes this point when he says, "a second strike capability helps in stabilizing the first strike capability. Therefore, at some point in time, Pakistan should be looking at a second strike capability." However, he also clarified that it need not necessarily be submarine-based, and could also be a limited one.[81]

From CMD to full-spectrum deterrence: Like the Indian deterrent's "credibility" and "minimum" being dynamically subjected to the capability acquisition by China, Pakistan's pursuit of CMD has never remained static owing to the consistent expansion of the Indian arsenal. While Pakistani officials have

---

80 Pakistan made this announcement in 2012, on the sidelines of the inauguration of the Naval Strategic Forces headquarters, which also underlined the creation of service specific strategic forces command as a symbol of dispersing nuclear assets to all the three services. The press release from Inter-Services Public Relations said: "HQ NSFC will perform a pivotal role in the development and employment of the Naval Strategic Force . . . which is the custodian of the nation's 2nd strike capability." See, "Naval Chief Inaugurates Naval Strategic Forces Headquarters," Islamabad, 19 May 2012, at http://www.ispr. gov.pk/front/main.asp?o=t-press_release&id=2067, accessed June 2012.

81 It is assumed that the second strike capability will be centred on the *Agosta* submarines, though there are no clear indications yet about whether missile systems will see naval variants for the SLBM platforms.

always asserted that the "precise numbers cannot be quantified", or that "the size of the arsenal and its deployment pattern have to be adjusted to ward off dangers of pre-emption and interception,"[82] the "minimum" has been subjected to sustained "qualitative and quantitative adjustments" in recent years because of reasons such as India's massive conventional build up; the India-US nuclear deal; its pursuit of a missile defence system; and new military doctrines.[83] However, the heightened expansion of the arsenal in the last one decade, especially after the Indo-US nuclear deal was announced, signifies a prominent shift in Pakistan's nuclear posture, which Pakistani officials term as full-spectrum deterrence. Kidwai explains the shift thus:

> The program is not open-ended. It started with a concept of credible minimum deterrence, and certain numbers were identified, and those numbers were achieved not too far away in time. Then we translated it to the concept of full-spectrum deterrence, which was the response to plugging those gaps which were bothering or driving the Cold Start Doctrine in identifying those gaps etc. Therefore, a certain degree of dynamism came into the program. And to cover the different additions that demanded of full spectrum deterrence, the numbers were modified.

The shift to "full spectrum deterrence" largely implies three consequences: (a) expansion of capabilities to cater to the full spectrum of theatres (which drove the initial posture); (b) the development of new nuclear thresholds and response options that could yield the postural advantage that Pakistan held in the early years of covert nuclearisation, though capability-driven rather than behaviour-driven; and (c) enhance the credibility of the deterrent through systems for each threat scenarios, instead of flexible numbers. According to Naeem Salik, it is a matter of time before Pakistan has the building blocks of full spectrum deterrence, with

---

82 See Agha Shahi, Zulfiqar Ali Khan and Abdul Sattar, "Securing Nuclear Peace," *The News*, 5 October 5 1999.

83 Memorandum from Air Commodore Khalid Banuri, Director of Arms Control and Disarmament Affairs in the SPD to CRS in December 2011. See, Paul K. Kerr and Mary Beth Nikitin, "Pakistan's Nuclear Weapons," *Congressional Research Service Report* (RL34248), 14 January 2016.

missile systems in sufficient number both at the shortest- and longest-range ends, to put full spectrum deterrence into practice.[84] However, he cautions that Pakistan cannot convert full-spectrum posture into a nuclear warfighting capability as this involves battlefield targeting that demands a larger arsenal size, a greater variety of warheads-delivery combine, and comparatively higher operational preparedness, all of which are currently constrained by resources and political constraints.

For leading Pakistani voices like Kidwai, the quest for full-spectrum was essentially driven by India's projection of the Cold Start/pro-active doctrine which prompted the development of the *Nasr* tactical nuclear system. Kidwai insists that *Nasr* was born out of India's attempts to find space for conventional war despite Pakistan's nuclear weapons because a gap existed due to the absence of a complete spectrum of deterrence. Yet, the actual meaning for this posture is driven by what some Pakistani analysts' term as "nuclear weapons of all descriptions in the arsenal to provide full spectrum deterrence"—tactical nuclear weapons at the lowest level, a second strike capability by equipping conventional submarines with nuclear-tipped missiles, and cruise missiles to beat the Indian BMDs.[85] Such expansive deterrent structuring is also driven by the fact that India has signalled its refusal to endorse a tactical nuclear warfighting theatre, and is going ahead with ostensible plans for a nation-wide defence that could complement its massive retaliation posturing.

Pakistan's Response to Indian BMD

India's missile defence capability creates numerous challenges for Pakistan's deterrence. First, India could gear up to neutralise or limit damage from a Pakistani conventional or nuclear first strike with its missile defence systems, and then initiate a massive retaliation which could lead to the major destruction of Pakistan depending on the nature of the strike. Second, India could embark

---

84 See Salik, n.70.

85 See Tasleem, n.69.

on a pre-emptive strike against Pakistan's counter-force and counter-military assets, and protect its core assets against potential retaliation if Pakistan manages to secure or develop second-strike components for retaliation. Third, India could also consider the forward deployment of lower-tier BMD or augmented air defences to support its strike-corps thrusts to intercept Pakistan's tactical systems.

Thus, Pakistan does not view India's missile defence capability in isolation, but conceives the threat envelope in conjunction with Cold Start; this, in fact, prompts the full-spectrum deterrence pursuit. This is beside a diplomatic campaign to demonize Cold Start as driving its security dilemma and causing instability in the region; enhancing its fissile production as a response to the advantage India gains in its fissile stocks through the India-US nuclear deal; and also cite the Indian missile defence as a destabilizing factor.[86] The significant aspect, however, is that Pakistan also conceives of its full-spectrum capabilities to provide it with a denial deterrence posture. Many Pakistani analysts believe that the combined application of the *Nasr* tactical system with the two land-attack and air-launched cruise missiles of *Babar* and *Ra'ad* (both specifically developed to defeat missile shields) will provide Pakistan with a denial deterrence capability, and aggravate the operational spectrum for Indian conventional strategies.[87]

While the success of such perceptive strategies may be left to actual operational realities, the fact remains that Pakistan has not found suitable technological responses to the Indian missile defence capability. It could be logically assumed that Pakistan could also adopt a response strategy like that of many other nuclear-armed states which have been confronted with a monopolistic BMD acquisition by a rival state. The initial

---

86 Pakistan reportedly opposed BMD deployments in the CBM talks with India, besides highlighting it as part of India's offensive build-up. See, ISPR Press Release of 16ᵗʰ NCA Meeting, January 13, 2010, at http://www.ispr.gov.pk/ front/main.asp?o=t-press_release&date=2010/1/13, accessed August 2013.

87 See Salik, n.70.

reactions of Russia and China to the US East European BMD plan and theatre defence in East Asia were more about resisting the deployments, citing their instability factor. Russia initially talked about the mass deployment of its advanced ICBMs (like *Topol-M*) in order to overwhelm American interceptors, while China used the US BMD as another reason to hasten the modernization of its strategic forces, besides hinting at the development of counter-measures to beat the US BMD. Over the years, both ended up developing advanced theatre defences and pursuing systems that could mimic the mid-course interceptors in the US inventory.

The case of Pakistan might be no different. It started out by citing the destabilising quotient of Indian missile defences, and then went on to develop cruise missiles as anti-BMD platforms, and then vied to project the pursuit of a potential denial deterrence plan. Certainly, it might be a matter of time before Pakistan either pursues a missile defence capability or seeks external technological assistance, as has been the constant signature of its nuclear and missile programmes. In the current scheme of things, Pakistan has only a rudimentary air defence capability (comprising of the *Spada 2000*, and a recent acquisition of LOMADS LY80).[88] Though there are no current indications about a potential development programme for strategic interceptors—considering that Pakistan has a formidable missile technology infrastructure to support its frontline strategic missile forces, and has been able to successfully develop tactical delivery systems and cruise missile in a small window—it could be difficult to dismiss the probability of Pakistan already considering the option of indigenously developing missile defence platforms. Even if success evades this potential mission, Pakistan could fall back upon China to acquire advanced air defence systems (the *Hongqi* series) and, later, maybe even seek the transfer of advanced interceptors through the existing technological partnerships facilitated by their "all-weather" friendship. A probable or eventual acquisition of missile defence capability by Pakistan would have multiple effects: it

---

88 "Army inducts air defence system to enhance ability," *Pakistan Today*, 12 March 2017.

may regain confidence well enough to further alter or expand its deterrence structures and postures in a manner that could support its political objectives vis-à-vis the strategic competition with India; it could also use the defensive parity to work on deterrence stability with India. Whether it is the latter option or the total absence of options, another deterrence churning might certainly be in store.

CHAPTER - VI

CONCLUSION

Security dilemmas are dynamic and uncontrolled processes, often assumed to be caused by offensive postures. However, as this volume has attempted to show, they could also be caused by the introduction of defensive systems with inherent characteristics to complement the offensive intentions. Thus, competitions will continue to define strategic equations and potentially heighten arms races, which though could progressively lead to new stability arrangements, driven by the fact that nuclear wars are sought to be avoided by all nations. All efforts for security maximization are eventually driven by this sole consideration, but pursued with varied objectives of dissuasion, denial, and deterrence. Nations are prompted to seek security through their perceptions of offence, defence, or a combination of both. Missile defences come into this picture with the potential for all these utilities. In the process, missile defences emerge as security maximisers; but if their applications and resultant equations are prudently managed, these systems could also evolve into security stabilizers.

As this study has argued, missile defences could promote a defensive balance by increasing the relative costs of aggression, though also encourage belligerence by the states possessing them. The positive side of its acquisition could, however, be highlighted by the fact that countries pursuing this technology evidently seek to enhance their defensive capability, and calibrate their deterrence systems so as to deny opportunities of intimation and threat. A balancing of offensive and defensive capabilities could be treated with optimism if, in the long run, it favours strategic stability and convince nations on the futility of building up offensive forces. Ultimately, the balance of capabilities and postures, and the causal for stability will be determined by how countries prefer to adopt defensive balancing and abhor instruments and policies of expansion and aggression. One could hope that BMD systems will emerge as an ideal technological catalyst for a future of strategic stability.

The previous chapter undertook a detailed case study of the Southern Asian theatre, marked for the presence of two competing dyads, and the dynamic state of deterrence prevailing in both dyads. The attempt there was to understand how missile defence could influence or impact the deterrence structures in a region with multiple nuclear-armed states, and how their deterrence structures have to adapt to the increasing influence of missile defence capabilities, howsoever asymmetric they remain. This theatre is a unique mix: on the one hand is the dominant nuclear power China, which has a consolidated nuclear deterrence posture vis-à-vis its neighbours; on the other are India and Pakistan whose deterrence structures continue to be in various evolutionary stages and throw up numerous possibility of instability. The imbalance, uncertainty or inconsistency of deterrence in this region could be attributed to a multiplicity of its primary actors as well as to secondary (and extra-regional) influences. The chapter showed how BMD technology, despite being premature in terms of development and by its role in the deterrence churning has, nevertheless, begun to affect the region's strategic dynamics. However, its full dimensions are yet to be comprehended, which shows in the lack of its assimilation in the doctrinal structures of both India and China. Both nations are yet to grapple with the complete dimensions of this technology, and integrate it into their deterrent structures. Yet, their preliminary posturing itself has menaced their adversaries or forced them to revisit their postures, which could be an empirical commentary on the offence-defence balance.

While missile defence is likely to further stabilize the already balanced nuclear deterrence equation in the China-India dyad, notwithstanding the asymmetry of offensive forces, the case of the India-Pakistan dyad is evidence of how one party (India) has used missile defence as a countervailing force against nuclear blackmail and brinkmanship, and also to mitigate the exploitation of the vacuum created by a lopsided doctrinal framework. The consequential pursuit of "deterrence by denial" by both actors in this dyad, even if through different approaches, generates scope for incremental progress towards stability, with the lessening space for escalation indicating the compounding effect BMD could have on deterrence. Considering that this technology is still evolving, there is a possibility that more sweeping transformations might be in store when BMD systems are operationalised across the region. Its strategic dimensions could probably turn out to be far more intense and sweeping than is currently perceived. It may possibly lead to a new environment of deterrence stability and offence-defence balancing between China and India, and potential postural shifts in Pakistan's nuclear behaviour. At the same time, the possibility of a new wave of strategic arms competition cannot be ruled out if security dilemmas persist, and the introduction of missile defences continues to aggravate rather than diminish them.

On a global scale, the recent demonstrations of interception tests by both China and India, and the publicising of a long-held capability by Russia, is testament to the fact that more and more nuclear-armed states will find missile defence an effective means to plug traditional insecurities associated with keeping vulnerabilities open, and also to address the conventional problem of maintaining deterrence credibility. In many ways, it reinforces the framework propounded by US President George W. Bush (Jr.) in 2001 of comprehensive defence where offensive forces are complemented by defensive depth as a means to depart from Cold War era dimensions of mutual vulnerability. On the other hand, there is a lack of conceptual clarity on how these nuclear-armed powers are seeking to project their missile defence capability — either in conjunction with offensive forces to add value to the net deterrence posture, or as a certain means to move away from offensive posturing and seek a defensive balance. In fact, the coming strategic dimension of missile defences will largely be based on which of these options the nuclear powers will resort to.

Despite claims of protecting the US homeland with a nation-wide defensive shield and complementing extended deterrence through the forward deployment of strategic interceptors and theatre defences in allied territory, the American security establishment seems to harbour beliefs of these systems providing an additional deterrence edge vis-à-vis nuclear rivals. While its primary rivals, the Russians and Chinese, intend to mimic the US strategy, there seems to be greater realisation among the three major nuclear powers on the diminished space for conflict escalation to nuclear levels, howsoever limited the current theatres of military confrontation, as a direct implication of the defensive depth provided by the mass deployment of these systems. Thus, it might not be inappropriate to infer the prospective spin-offs of such strategic stabilising effects on nuclear reductions and disarmament initiatives, though their eventual outcome will be determined by the nature of the emerging race in defensive platforms, and how the posturing is intended by the possessing states.

This book has aspired to provide a basic discursive structure for these questions to be examined and addressed by using the offence-defence balance framework. The objective was to create a basic conceptual environment to explore whether this framework is best suited to explain the impact of missile defences on nuclear deterrence, either by imparting an offensive edge to the possessing state and adding to its net deterrence, or by creating a defensive balance that could address vulnerabilities and credibility gaps traditionally associated with deterrence. While technology has been a key variable used by theorists to explain the dynamics of the offence-defence balance in strategic relationships, this study hopes to set the ground for further investigations and debates in this direction by applying missile defences as the case study to examine the scope and feasibility of the technological variable, or its explanatory potential for the offence-defence balance framework.

INDEX

A

Advanced Air Defence (AAD) ix, 101

Advanced Technology Vessel (ATV) xx

Agni xix, xx, 83, 84, 93, 97, 98, 99, 101, 102

Airborne Laser (ABL) xix, 18, 22, 30

Almaz-Antey Corporation xvi

Alternative Infrared Satellite System (AIRSS) 23

Anti-Ballistic Missile (ABM) x, 1, 14

Anti-Ballistic Missile Treaty of 1972 2

Anti-Nuclear Strategic Defence 1

Anti-Satellite (ASAT) 17, 27

Arihant xx, 98

B

Ballistic Missile Defence (BMD) i, iii, xii, xviii, 1, 8, 9, 15, 39, 84, 85, 105

Ballistic Missile Defence Review (BMDR) xviii

BMD in the South Asian Nuclear Dynamics 52

BMD in US Deterrence Postures 51

BMD platforms xvii, 84, 116

Boost Phase Interception (BPI) 15

C

Carl von Clausewitz 55

Carnegie Nuclear Policy Conference xii

Chemical oxygen-iodine laser (COIL) 22

Cimbala, Stephen 4

Cold War viii, x, xi, 2, 5, 7, 8, 9, 17, 24, 29, 34, 36, 38, 40, 42, 43, 45, 46, 47, 51, 59, 65, 75, 120

Countering America's Adversaries Through Sanctions Act (CAATSA) xv

D

Defence Research Development Organisation (DRDO) 98

Democratic Peoples' Republic of North Korea (DPRK) 44

Deng Xiaoping 74

Dhanush 98

E

Early Launch Detection and Tracking (ELDT) 35

Eastern European system 22

Exo-Atmospheric Kill Vehicle (EKV) 21

Exo-atmospheric Re-entry Vehicle Interceptor System (ERIS) 16

F

Freedman, Lawrence 6

G

Galosh A-350 interceptor 14

Geneva Disarmament Conference 61, 67

German Wasserfall 13

Ghauri-I 102

Ground-Based Interceptor (GBI) 16, 20

Ground-based Midcourse Defence System (GMDS) 8, 18

H

Hatf-10 111

High-Altitude Airship (HAA) 35

High Endo-atmospheric Defence Interceptor (HEDI) 16

High Energy Laser Mobile Demonstrator (HELMD) 31

High Energy Liquid Laser Area Defence System (HEL-LADS) 31

Hongqi system 27

I

Indian National Satellite System (INSAT) viii

Indian peaceful nuclear explosion (PNE) 92

Indian Pugwash Society viii

Indian Remote Sensing (IRS) vii

Indian Space Research Organisation (ISRO) vii

Integrated Guided Missile Development Programme (IGMDP) xx, 97

Inter-Continental Ballistic Missiles (ICBMs) 59, 76

J

Johnston, Alastair 76, 82

K

Kinetic Energy Interceptor (KEI) 30, 32

Kinetic Kill Vehicle (KKV) 32

L

Long Range Surface-to-Air Missile (LRSAM) 27

M

Mao Zedong 74

Mutual Assured Destruction (MAD) 2

N

National Defence Authorisation Act (NDAA) xvi

National Missile Defence (NMD) viii, 3, 8

No-First-Use (NFU) 72, 77, 89

Non-Proliferation of Nuclear Weapons (NPT) 62

Nuclear Posture Review (NPR) xviii

O

Operation Parakram 90, 91

Over-the-Horizon Radar (OTHR) 35

P

Prithvi ix, xix, 97, 98, 101, 102, 103, 124

Prithvi Air Defence ix, 101

Prithvi Air Defence Experiment (PADE) 101

R

Russian S-400 system xiii

S

Sagarika xx, 98

Satellite Launch Vehicle (SLV) vii

Sea-Based Anti-Ballistic Missile Intercept System (SABMIS) 30

Shaheen-II 102

Shaheen III 103

Skyguard systems 36

Sky Shield 36

Space-Based Interceptor (SBI) 16

Star Wars x, xiv, 5

Strategic Arms Limitation Talks (SALT-I) 2

Strategic Defence Initiative (SDI) x, xix, 2

Strategic Forces Command (SFC) 98, 104

Strategic Plans Division (SPD) xii

Submarine-Launched Ballistic Missiles (SLBMs) 59, 76

Surgical Strikes 92

T

Theatre High Altitude Area Defence (THAAD) xvii, xviii, 16, 17, 18, 19, 20, 32,

80, 105

Theatre Missile Defence (TMD)
viii, 73

Thumba Equatorial Rocket
Launching Station
(TERLS) vii

Topol-M ICBM 52

Trump's BMD policy xviii

U

United Nations Outer Space
Treaty 34

Upgraded Early Warning Radars
(UEWRs) 23

US Project Plato 13

V

Vikram Sarabhai Space Centre
(VSSC) vii

W

Weapons of Mass Destruction
(WMD) 19